Developed Minds, Developing Minds and the Stupid Terrorists

Harish Maiya

Author's Note/Acknowledgements

Although the idea to write this book happened overnight a long time ago, it took a while to compile everything and make it what it is now. In the process, I put a lot of people including my family and friends through hardship, but I promised them everything would return to normal at least until I wake up one day to work on the next book. When the Lufthansa flight landed at the Dallas airport on a cold rainy evening in January 1998, it never occurred to me I would be writing a book one day. Landing in the United States for the first time, all my twenty-three-year-old brain could think of was chasing the American dream and chasing beautiful girls that I have been doing ever since.

Thanks to my family for not giving up on me and thanks to my friends for their consistent support over the years. A round of applause to the hard-working editorial team at BookSurge for their efforts to make it happen. Last but not least, thanks to the amazing baristas at Starbucks who managed to keep my inspirations high, even when a lot of caffeine would not do the trick.

Contents

Introduction: The potential of the human mind is second only to Mother Nature, but the individual must decide how to use it and to what extent. Most people utilize only up to five percent of their brain's capacity; but if we utilized 100 percent, the human race would be pretty close to being powerful as Autobots and Decepticons. Being a social creature, we tend to use most of the power residing inside the skull for mundane activities. Evolving from a reptilian brain and then a mammalian brain, the human brain is a complex structure with complex processes. Of the six or more billion people living in this world, some are developed minds, some are developing minds, and the rest are categorized as underdeveloped minds. Developed minds are the minds that constructively use their brainpower to its maximum extent and to the highest standards; developed minds include the founding fathers and visionaries of developed countries. These minds have the capability to give attention to detail while thinking about critical issues, have the most positive impact, raise the bar and add value to people and societies. The developed minds live life to the fullest while still trying to bring the best out in everyone around them. Developing minds use their brainpower constructively but not to the maximum extent and not to the highest standards. Underdeveloped minds–including the stupid terrorists–barely use their brainpower for any constructive cause and get entangled in issues that have a negative impact to society. With that said, a developed mind has room to improve, a developing mind definitely needs to improve and the underdeveloped ones need serious help!

From the early manifestation of Homo sapiens, human minds and societies have evolved through discoveries and inventions–sometimes gradual and sometimes by quantum leaps–starting with the development of simple modes of communication and writing after the agricultural revolution, which resulted in civilization. Agricultural civilizations like the Sumerian, Egyptian, and Harappan civilizations were scattered around rivers and lakes and led to the discovery of primitive transportation systems. The conflicts between them gave rise to cities-states, empires, and eventually to countries. As these civilizations grew, there was a need for public safety and security that led to the formation of governments. As the economic system grew, the need for governments increased due to the increased pursuit of the seven deadly sins by the public. The Middle Ages saw quite a few inventions in a number of areas and also saw the establishment of universities in major European cities. This period saw advancement in medicine, the introduction of the decimal system, invention of algebra and enormous development in the fields of art, sculpture, music and architecture. The twelfth and thirteenth centuries saw significant changes in Europe, with the introduction of new ways of managing production and economic growth. The rate of technological innovations increased including the introduction of the cannon, spectacles, artesian wells, gunpowder, and silk. The invention of the compass and major enhancements to ships and clocks led to the beginning of the age of exploration. This exploration spanned two centuries starting in the fifteenth century when Europeans traveled around the world in ships, which could even safely sail the Atlantic Ocean, looking for trading partners and commodities like gold, silver, and spices. The age of exploration also led Europeans to the Americas, which were abundant with resources like gold that encouraged continued emigration of Europeans. During this time of exploration, inventions like printers and the printing press revolutionized bookmaking all over Europe, ending the Middle Ages and leading to the Renaissance and scientific revolution.

During the scientific revolution, many noted scientists and inventors were devout in their faith but others questioned the power of religion largely because of contradictions between ideas supported by religion and those supported by science. At this time the Greek and Roman societies had an advanced economy, with financial markets and private-property rights that helped build capital along with increased productivity. The theoretical scientific revolution had little immediate, practical technological impact on societies until the eighteenth century, when the accumulation of knowledge and technology reached its peak and initiated a flurry of practical inventions. These scientific advances ultimately led to the Industrial Revolution.

The domination of European societies as compared to some Asian societies was due to their stronger work ethic combined with restrained population growth. Celibate clergy, warfare, the outbreak of the bubonic plague that wiped out about 50 percent of the population of Europe and late marriages—all led to controlled population growth in Europe.

On the Indian subcontinent during the Indus Valley civilization and subsequently, even though the economy was self-sufficient, much of it was controlled by social restrictions put in place by the class system. During the eighteenth century and the early part of the nineteenth century, India suffered as a silver-standard economy trading with gold-standard countries, but it was still the second largest economy after China. The latter part of the nineteenth century saw the rise of the United Kingdom and the United States, as well as a number of other European countries due to the Industrial Revolution in Europe. As the British rule started in India, so did its economic decline compared to other industrialized economies. India was also in the forefront of science and technology, but its unresolved social issues and poorly formed government made it impossible to move forward.

While some developed and developing minds show an extreme level of greed for money, the underdeveloped terrorists show fanatic levels of wrath, envy, and greed for control. They all need to be controlled by the mainstream society by exerting moderation and bringing into life the concept of share and prevail. There has been opposition to governments, regulations, and authority but having a strong and effective government is required for the continuous growth of the human race. Without strong, effective government, chaos that will ultimately lead to the destruction of the human race ensues. While kingdoms were a raw form of government, democratically elected governments are more seasoned; a developed one will take care of its people much better than a developing or an underdeveloped one. The governments in the developed world are willing and have the ability to put a check on people that go too far with greed, but many developing and underdeveloped governments are unstable and unable to systematically check on its people. In spite of the level of greed for money displayed by some developed minds, they are the most generous in terms of charitable giving. U.S. citizens top the list giving away almost $300 billion in 2006. Some developed governments in Europe compensate for the lack of charitable giving by their citizens by increasing their direct aid to developing and underdeveloped countries. Apart from the fanatic levels of wrath, envy, and greed for control displayed by the underdeveloped terrorists, their restless blood is boiling with vengeance. The only way for them to fit into the mainstream society is to learn and educate themselves. If they don't make changes to refurbish themselves, their lives will be an insignificant loss to the mainstream society.

Chapter 1

How We Got Here

If only Christopher Columbus had correctly identified the new land he discovered, this continent would have been named after him. Instead, Amerigo Vespucci realized that he hadn't reached Asia but a new continent. Although a number of Europeans emigrated to the Americas to make use of the rich natural resources, rivers, and diverse climate, rapid economic and technological advancement happened only between the eighteenth and twentieth centuries. During this time, with enormous leadership from the founding fathers and great visionaries, the United States was transformed from an agricultural economy to an industrial power of the world that surpassed its European counterparts. Five years after the American colonies gained independence, transportation infrastructure growth and technological innovation fueled industrial output. Both Columbus and Vespucci would be so proud of their discovery of America because of the transformation this country has been able to make in the political and economic landscape for the rest of the world.

Most developing countries, even after decades of independence still lack the infrastructure needed to take the next big economic step. Forefathers of the developing and underdeveloped worlds would not be so proud to see the growth or decline of their countries since some of them are hell bent on destroying it. Both World Wars together resulted in over one hundred million deaths and significant damage to the economy and infrastructure in Europe. But they got right back up, whereas the Indian subcontinent has been struggling with wars against neighbors and mired in sociopolitical complexities. The Indian subcontinent has been constantly changing and evolving but not as fast as their European counterparts who have evolved tremendously since the scientific revolution. Although the Indian Constitution abolished the caste system—believed by researchers to being established by the Indo-Aryans—, remnants of it are still seen in society. The caste system may have worked to its advantage in ancient self-reliant social structure but would not work in a modern economic and social structure. The government has initiated a new system of reservations by which the Dalits and other minorities are offered special admission to schools, universities, and public service jobs based only on their caste and not merit, This could work for the short term but would be a disaster in the long run. Merit should be considered for reservations especially in fields like medicine if India wants to be in par with the developed world.

Technological advancement has both constructive and destructive efforts—one of the reasons why Autobots need to always have an upper hand over the Decepticons. The two world superpowers, along with their allies, engaged in a cold war filled with tension and competition from the 1940s until the 1990s. There was tension due to military buildup that usually proved costly, political tussles, propaganda, and espionage, whereas competition was healthy with industrial and technological advancements. The cold war military expenditure for the United States was an enormous eight trillion dollars, including weapons research and spending on nuclear stockpiles as part of the nuclear arms race between the two superpowers. During and after the cold war, it was Russia acting as the Decepticons, whereas the United States was acting as the Autobots, making sure they would be able to defend themselves and their allies in case of an invasion. On the positive side, the United States and the Soviet Union were competing in the space race, which created incredible advancements in science and technology. The U.S. space race led to an emphasis on education in these areas and increased government funding for these programs.

While the developed world is already working on making the International Space Station the next commercial tourist destination, the developing world is concentrating on practical space missions and research that it considers beneficial to people in terms of remote sensing and communications. Even though the Indian government woke up to space research just ten years after gaining its independence from the British when Russia successfully launched Sputnik, its space research has been really slow due to bureaucracy, corruption, and lack of skills. India successfully launched a satellite through its first homegrown Satellite Launch Vehicle (SLV) in 1980, but by that time the space race between the two superpowers had ended. It's not just the amount of research in various fields that distinguishes the developed minds from the developing minds but also the ability to think ahead. Developed minds pursue research in various fields like alternative energy, fuel, and medicine to develop the next generation of technology and processes that will significantly improve human development and existence, while adhering to the highest level of environmental standards.

During the cold war, the United States was home to a number of game-changing inventions like the polio vaccine, integrated circuit, operating system, minicomputer, calculator, laser, and optical fiber. In the 1980s, the invention of the TCP/IP protocol led to the birth of the Internet or the World Wide Web, which is used by more than a third of the world's population. Who would have thought researchers would be able to grow stem cells in their lab to find treatments to a number of diseases? These cures will one day be available to the general public at a reasonable cost and have incredible effects. There were a number of American inventors during the eighteenth, nineteenth, and twentieth centuries that have changed our everyday lives and the way people do business. Although there have been a number of great theoretical inventions and discoveries in various fields by Indians, the lack of practical inventions and inventions of quantum leaps have made it difficult for India to keep up with the United States and Europe in terms of quality, quantity, and significance of its inventions.

A good analogy for the differences in the developed and the developing world would be the race between the computer manufacturing giant Intel and its underdog competitor AMD. Although at times in the business cycle, Intel, which enjoys more than a 70 percent market share, seems like it's losing its grip, it bounces back due to its enormous pool of technical resources and huge cash flow. Whenever its competitors come up with a good design and seem to have the upper hand, Intel retaliates with an even better design that not only wins customers back but also attracts new customers. With its vast technical resources and superior marketing capabilities, Intel also moved to provide complete platform solutions to customers giving it an edge that its competitors were unable to provide. A number of developing countries have been labeled emerging markets because of their economic significance, but the underdog developing world has not had as much luck as AMD in competing with the developed world for a number of reasons.

Indian mathematicians like Aryabhata and Ramanujan and physicists like C.V. Raman and Homi J. Bhabha have made some contributions in their areas of research, but they aren't close to the game-changing, practical inventions of the developed world. The disparity is readily apparent in winners of the coveted Nobel Prize for outstanding contributions in the fields of physics, chemistry, literature, peace, economics, and physiology or medicine. Since the award was first given in 1901, hundreds of people from the developed world have been awarded the Nobel Prize, including over 300 citizens of the United States. Fewer than ten people from India have won the Nobel Prize. The ratio of prizewinners from the developed world to that in the developing world is even larger when one considers the three coveted awards for mathematical contributions namely the Wolf Prize, Fields Medal and the Abel Prize.

Lack of practical inventions in the developing world is due to a number of socioeconomic reasons, with economic reasons including insufficient government funding for research and development in universities and lack of private sector investment for research and development. The developed world should take advantage of the developing world's talent pool and lower costs and significantly increase its investment in research and development in the developing world. A number of social reasons hinder progress: priority is given to religion, social status, and family; lack of visionaries to focus on the big picture; a lack of support for the existent; and the educated breadwinner chooses a higher paying job rather than one in research or development. Priority given to family involves working to only satisfy the needs of the family, rather than working to unleash one's full potential. Priority given to religion involves a number of religiously inclined people with a number of superstitions focused on the nation's rich history and heritage; this makes them reluctant to adapt to change. Even the few visionaries in the government and public sector are restricted by the dirty political activities of the coalition central government. If people were ready to adapt to change and somebody gave the government and each citizen a plan for becoming a developed nation, even if only one-quarter of the citizenry followed the process, there would be drastic changes for the better. But since such a process does not exist, it won't happen and even if it exists, it would take a long time for developing countries to cultivate the process.

Documentary filmmakers like Michael Moore are rare in developing countries, where documentaries, although popular for delving into critical, everyday topics, have been controversial. Moore has made documentaries on good topics like American's corporate culture, gun culture, healthcare system, and the face of capitalism during an economic downturn. But he always depicts these topics so negatively, sometimes even manipulating facts to his advantage, that people praise him as a hero for going against these systems. In 2003, Moore made his most controversial and most popular documentary *Fahrenheit 9/11*, which addresses ties between former President George W. Bush and the bin Laden family of Saudi Arabia and the U.S. war on terrorism, especially the invasions of Afghanistan and Iraq. The bin Laden family and the Saudi government had severed ties with radical terrorist Osama bin Laden way before 2001 because of Osama's rebellion against the Saudi government's ties with Western states. Moore alleges that the U.S. government evacuated members of the bin Laden family from the U.S. on a secret flight right after the September 2001 attacks on the World Trade Center. The nature of the attacks and the ties between the U.S. and Saudi governments, it would be normal to provide extra security to the bin Laden family in the United States. These allegations by Moore in the documentary are believed to be inaccurate and baseless, which made it controversial and popular— it grossed over $200 million at the box office. Moore's allegation that the United States began the war in Afghanistan to fulfill its ulterior motive— acquiring a natural gas pipeline—is on par with his ulterior motive of amassing money by making such controversial films based on allegations mired with inaccuracies. Moore alleges that the U.S. government induced a climate of fear among the U.S. population through the media and its antiterrorism efforts were intended to expand the government's power. Moore needs to see that the U.S. government was only trying to prevent another attack by the radical terrorists by keeping the public alert and aware of their surroundings. What would one rather have—a little invasion of privacy by the government or another attack by the stupid terrorists? Don't believe everything in his documentaries because he cherry-picks his subjects and manipulates his scenes to make it controversial and hence a moneymaker. He is a for-profit filmmaker who happens to select interesting topics and depict them in a way that maximizes profits.

If Moore really is interested in bringing change to the issues he addresses in his documentaries, why doesn't he give away those hundreds of millions of dollars in profits to charities that work toward those goals? Moore should really walk the walk and not just talk the talk because his only charitable contribution is a $10 thousand donation to an anti-Moore campaigner to make him shut up. Although most Americans agree that the war in Iraq was not necessary, they generally agree that strong and stable democratic governments in those regions will result in a peaceful region, which will help stabilize the price of various commodities like oil.

In the big picture, if the already crumbling regime of Saddam had not been brought down completely, he and his notorious sons would be making their people suffer in terror and poverty while they continued to live lavishly, developing and using chemical and other weapons of mass destruction and creating an unstable region and economy. An interesting analogy would be when Tiger Woods and his coach started working to change his swing; some analysts called it the downfall of Tiger as he was having some trouble. But in the big picture, Tiger and his coach were working on a long-term strategy and a swing that would work for Tiger in the long run. It did, and he is still winning more trophies than any other current PGA professional. So should the long-term strategy in Iraq, which does not mean U.S. soldiers and officials need to be present in Iraq for a long-term to make it a success.

A developed country is made up of developed economies, with high human development index, high per capita income and a developed industrial base. Whereas a developing country is defined as one with relatively low standard of living, moderate human development index, moderate per capita income, and an underdeveloped industrial base. These quantitative indices measure developed and developing countries, and the underlying qualitative facts are very high for a developed country and low for a developing country, along with the quantitative indices that go hand in hand. Since the quantitative indices and the underlying qualitative facts go hand in hand, for a developing country like India, even though the quantitative indices have been increasing, the qualitative facts have not changed. This makes it hard for India to move from a developing country to a developed country.

The other factor is the increase in population; India is closing in on China's population. For a developing country like India, the standard of living has increased in big cities and smaller towns due to substantial rise in the numbers of rich and the middle class citizens. This is offset by the vast numbers of people in villages who are still uneducated and base their livelihood on agriculture and farming. These farmers have really hard times to make ends meet due to poor yields because of poor operating tools. To develop, India needs to move away from low-value-adding sectors like agriculture, which will happen when more people get an education and put their education to use by working in an industry. The human development index, which is a measure of life expectancy, literacy, education, and GDP per capita has increased substantially because of the rise in income for the middle class and the rich, which has allowed more education and which in turn has increased the life expectancy. Countries with a human development index score of over 0.8 are considered to have a high standard of human development. India currently has a human development index of about 0.6. Although traveling around the country, this number may seem to be a little high for the state of affairs in a number of towns and villages across the country. The developed economies and industrial base is due to the existence of services sectors like wholesale, retail, entertainment, news media, health care and leisure/hotel. It is also due to the existence of intellectual services like information genera-tion/sharing, education and research/development.

The other important tenet displayed by the citizens of the developed world is secular humanism, something that greatly helps increase the hu-man development index. A conviction to test political or social beliefs; a commitment to use scientific methods of inquiry; a primary concern with fulfillment, growth, and creativity; a concern and commitment to making this life meaningful; and a conviction to building a better world are all part of the secular humanism. In contrast, people in developing nations typically embrace religious humanism. Religious humanism may provide intense reli-gious experiences to individuals that may enlighten and give personal satis-faction, but it lacks the social responsibilities and leadership that are required to enrich the human development index of a country or a region as a whole. The intelligence quotient of the people should be transformed to achieve higher human development index and greater personal and social meaning.

Although India has been termed as an emerging market by maintain-ing sustained economic growth and good economic potential, the industrial development that it should have seen is not happening because of poor execu-tion in infrastructure development, lack of a concrete education and welfare system, quick-changing, unstable governments that change its policies, rising demand in emerging markets that's increased the cost of real estate and raw materials, bureaucracy, and corruption. Most of the above reasons are due to poor work ethic shown by the political system and businesses. Even though the British ruled India for centuries and stole natural resources during that time, the progress after independence has been slow and cumbersome. In developed countries, corporations and the government invest a huge part of their revenue or budget in capital expenditure and research and development. Most of the universities in developed countries get grants from corporations and the government to conduct research. There is always encouragement to think outside the box and give awards for the next big achievement. For example, the Defense Advanced Research Projects Agency (DARPA) organizes an annual driverless car competition called the Grand Challenge among educational institution research teams. Held in the Mojave Desert, the Grand Challenge helps enrich and expand artificial intelligence research in the United States. DARPA is involved in the development of new technology, including computer networking, global positioning systems, the World Wide Web, and unmanned systems for military use. One would never see this kind of adventurous research project in India or anywhere in the developing world. Then there was the Ansari X Prize created by the X Prize Foundation that gave $10 million to any private organization that launched its creation into space and returned it to earth successfully. Mojave Aerospace Ventures, formed by Burt Rutan and Paul Allen, won this coveted space research prize. This private spacecraft innovation was a huge success since it cost about $30 million to build and launch; NASA spends billions of dollars to build and launch a space shuttle. That's the beauty of these competitions—it's all about the challenge and opportunity to invent something significant and worthwhile. If not, they wouldn't be spending $30 million to win $10 million. Following the X Prize competition, several companies have been offering commercial space flight for tourists with a lot of people already signing up for the ticket. The X Prize foundation along with Google have already setup the Google Lunar X Prize that awards $20 million to any privately funded team that successfully lands a robot on the moon that travels 500 meters over the lunar surface and sends images and data back to earth—all before end of 2012.

These examples clearly demonstrate the motivations of the private industry in the developed world that are usually not seen in the developing world. During the mid- to late-twentieth century, kids in developed nations were busy inventing electronic machines and computers, kids in developing countries were still stuck in the social stigma of nurturing their family's expectations and believing in the saying Curiosity killed the cat. Most of these incredible creations were the result of kids who had the revolutionary spirit of facilitating common people not of greed or ego; it was a bunch of geeks fiercely believing that computers and electronic devices would one day fit in everyone's living room, even when most people were not so sure. Also not seen in the developing world is active participation of people in the social causes in terms of volunteering opportunities that makes so much difference in the developed world every day. It is amazing to see a lot of people who move from a developing country to a developed country adapt to the new work culture, social life, and economy sooner or later.

So if we swap governments of a developing country and a developed country for a year or two or five, does that mean the developed country would transform into a developing country and the developing country into a developed country? I bet it would. So does that mean it's the system, the process, and the people who define a country as a developed country? Yes, for most of the part. It also depends on a strong and stable government, and an effective and sustainable financial system, along with a number of other factors. You may ask why India is still a developing country despite the fact that four of the top ten people on the 2008 Forbes world's billionaires list come from that country? And one of the top ten billionaires has a mansion worth $1 billion right next to a slum where more than 10 million people live in poor conditions. So the question to ask is what and where is the missing link?

Author Karl Albrecht in his book *Practical Intelligence* talks about existence of five types of intelligence—abstract intelligence, social intelligence, practical intelligence, emotional intelligence, aesthetic intelligence, and kinesthetic intelligence. He says society from a larger perspective, including parents, teachers, educators, professionals, executives and managers, consultants, legislators, political leaders, celebrities, and media leaders should promote the teaching, application, and appreciation of practical intelligence (PI) in our culture. As a developing country, the society should not only implement PI but all six intelligences to help them improve into a developed mind. To achieve this, developing countries should hire executive coaches from developed nations to study and provide the right guidance.

Albrecht writes about various kinds of thinkers called simplex thinkers, duplex thinkers, multiplex thinkers and omniplex thinkers. Here's an excerpt from his book:

Simplex thinkers out of fear and ignorance crave simple answers, simple worldviews, simple explanations, simple opinions, and simple solutions. They tend to be drawn toward powerful leader figures who promise them solutions to their lives' problems without taxing their gray matter. In primitive societies, simplex thinkers unquestioningly follow ancient beliefs and myths, rely on tradition and ritual to anesthetize their existential fears and ostracize or even kill others who differ with their beliefs and values. Simplex thinkers at the deepest levels of conviction — their religious beliefs — they are utterly convinced that their truth must be true for everybody. They don't understand that their religious beliefs, moral codes, social values and often their political convictions are largely an accident of space and time.

There are a number of simplex thinkers both in developed and developing countries, but there are more in developing countries. Simplex thinkers can be classified as simplex moderate thinkers and simplex radical thinkers, with moderate thinkers being more numerous. The simplex moderate thinkers go on to lead accomplished lives, with successful jobs, family, and friends, and aided by religious and nonreligious beliefs. Simplex radical thinkers, on the other hand, sometimes put their radical thinking to the test in negative terms and go down the path in society that no accomplished moderate thinker would intend to go.

Chapter 2

What's Government Got to Do with It?

What's a government got to do with it you ask? Believe it or not, a government has everything to do with whether a country is developed or not. Although the government may not be the only entity that creates a better path for a country's development, it is definitely a stepping-stone. A stable, independent, responsible, and powerful government that can strictly enforce laws is required for the better functioning of a country, and lack of such a government clearly differentiates the developed and the developing worlds. It also provides a clear picture of the great visionaries of the developed world versus the battle of dirty politics of the developing world. The great visionaries of the developed world continuously worked hard for the development of their country, while the leaders of the developing world were fighting for themselves—first with limited visions and actions for the country.

Throughout American history, politics has flourished under a two-party system, with the two dominant parties being the Democratic Party and the Republican Party. The Republican Party is defined as conservative and the Democratic Party as liberal, although individual members of both parties may have varied views and opinions. Indian politics has been a multiparty system, but recently many central and state governments are a coalition of more than two parties because without a clear majority, passing legislation was impossible. The current central government is made up of a coalition of twelve parties; the bureaucratic structure of the coalition government and the fickle mindedness of some of the parties in the coalition make it vulnerable to failure when one party withdraws from the coalition because of minor disputes. Whether it's the president or the prime minister, the vision and leadership of the government heads make a lot of difference to the country's outcome. Government leaders who understand the responsibility and the stake they hold will make the right decisions to take the country in the right direction. A stable and a great economy without a stable government may only see short-term success; to realize long-term success, a country needs a stable and independent government with leaders who can apply long-term vision for their country. Amazingly enough, one can see this difference in the government and their leaders between the developed and the developing world. Sometimes a great leader with a sub-par government or a sub-par leader with a great government team may not be able to demonstrate his or her full potential or even a great leader with a great government may not be able to cut it in a sub-par economy. In a developing country like India, a government may not be enough to change the shape and life of the over-populated country. Instead, a combination of things, including the people, must be in place.

Although the British ruled India for most modern time, its citizens and leaders had the opportunity to learn from the developed world. But even after more than six decades of freedom, that knowledge has hardly been put into practice. The common reasoning for this is the simplex mind of the people who tend to ask, "Why should we rule our country the way British did? Let's rule it our way even though it really sucks." The answer to the question is that one needs to change their simplex mindset and change the way they lead by looking at the way successful leaders put their dynamic mindset vision into action. Including the government, the entire country of India is like thousands of bats that fly fast in random directions but never collide. The government, the traffic, businesses, and the entire system work or seem to work in a delicate equilibrium amidst the utter chaos. One wrong move by a distracted or hesitant driver– be it the government, traffic, business–and all hell breaks loose for a while but recovers and gets back into the mode of delicate equilibrium in no time. Although not one leader can change everything and propose the best solutions for all issues, history has shown that various successful leaders in the United States have focused on one issue, maybe debt reduction or environment or social issues or infrastructure development, and made every successful effort to solve problems in that area. Whereas few leaders in India have made a successful attempt to solve one of the country's major issues, and the ones who attempted to focus on one issue got themselves mired in the petty politics played by the selfish but not-so-bright politicians of the government. In the United States, the core infrastructure development happened steadily over time because visionaries acted on various projects, including the interstate highways, transcontinental railroad, air traffic control system, dams, tunnels, and bridges that were way above par for their day and are continually being improved or kept current with technology. This never happens in a developing country like India because the government and the people don't give the highest preference to above par infrastructure development for a number of reasons. Even if any infrastructure development project gets the highest preference, it doesn't get finished above par because of poor planning and implementation, which can happen when everybody involved gives their 100 percent honest effort to provide the best finished product.

Most early presidents in the United States were passionate about building their country into an economic superpower and the later presidents realized the need to work hard to maintain that status. More than building an economic superpower, they were steadfast in establishing a free and independent democratic country that was favorable to its citizens. In contrast, socialist and communist countries not only built mediocre governments filled with chaos, their regulations were totally unfavorable to their citizens, resulting in people fleeing from the hold of their treacherous leaders. George Washington retired after leading the United States to defeat of the Kingdom of Great Britain in the American Revolutionary War but became the president two years later because he was zealous about building a great foundation for the country. Jawaharlal Nehru on the other hand worked hard along with Gandhi for India's independence from the British, but he was a supporter of Stalin and a firm believer in a gradually changing socialist government. While the leaders in the United States and most of the developed world created capitalist governments, implementing laws that they firmly believed in and resolving issues with a quick reflexes, leaders in the developing world established socialist governments that were slow to implement laws and resolve issues. Socialist governments in developing countries not only have a larger number of political issues that get the highest priority over the social and economic issues desired by the people. Considered one of the greatest U.S. presidents, Washington built a strong central government, implemented an effective tax system, created a national bank called the First Bank of the United States, and funded the national debt. Nehru regarded complete government control over industries as necessary compromise on quality and productivity.

In spite of creating the Planning Commission to charter investments in industries and agriculture, envisioning industries administered by the government with the purpose of serving public interest, India was plagued with poverty, unemployment, and food shortages. The Planning Commission should also have a plan B charter that would say if plan A has not worked and improved the situation in a decade, governments should be able to divert to plan B to make it work for the people. Nehru also introduced a number of social reforms, including establishing a number of educational institutions, and equality for women and scheduled castes, but sometimes it's not just about introducing reforms—it's important that they are the right reforms that would work best for the system. Thomas Jefferson, one of the most influential founding fathers and a political genius, created the Second Bank and funded the major improved interstate route called the National Road that spurred a number of technological innovations, including bridges of various architectural designs. He did this although he was opposed to corporations because he believed they challenged the government and the laws of the country. In his long public career, Jefferson frequently attempted to abolish or limit the advance of slavery, that including proposing a bill to ban further importation of slaves to the state of Virginia. Indira Gandhi, on the other hand, who served as India's prime minister for four terms, continuously used *Garibi Hatao* (Abolish Poverty) as her election campaign theme but did not deliver on her promises—only 4 percent of the economic development budget went toward abolishing poverty. While the American founding fathers took a conservative approach because of their fear of corruption, the socialist approach of the founding fathers of India often got them into trouble. This includes alleged malpractice involving election results for which Indira Gandhi advised the president to declare a state of emergency that continued for two years. There were mediocre government programs like Indira Gandhi's agricultural innovation programs and programs to battle malnutrition among kids that were successful but no ambitious projects like great political leader Abraham Lincoln's bill authorizing the heavily subsidized transcontinental railroad system. This grand railroad venture not only helped cut travel time between San Francisco and New York from months to a week, it also helped carry millions of dollars worth of freight across the country more cheaply. Those were the days when an U.S. president was powerful enough to enact anything that he truly believed in without any industry lobbyists or opposition party political strategists standing in the way.

Along with the railway acts, Lincoln was instrumental in implementing banking and various revenue acts and it is these game-changing infrastructure projects that a developing country needs to work on with planning and implementation that is on par with the projects implemented in the developed world. Even though the two leaders had different levels of visionary success and achievements, both were assassinated for their brave stance on one issue: Lincoln for abolishing slavery while providing the freedmen voting rights, and Gandhi for curbing militants in the Indian state of Punjab who were ridiculously asking for the creation of a separate country.

Theodore "Teddy" Roosevelt was one of the progressive reforming presidents who dissolved monopolistic corporations for illegal and corrupt practices, promoted a conservation movement to protect natural resources, and called for universal health care along with introduction of national health insurance. It is very disturbing to see that the United States has been trying to get into universal health care since Teddy but has been continuously thwarted by political and medical forces, especially doctors whose exorbitant incomes are threatened by universal healthcare. Does the United States need universal health care? Of course it does. It is not only about the forty or so million uninsured Americans but also the cost of health care, which is growing at a rate three times that of average wages. After Teddy, Harry Truman and then recently Bill Clinton tried to bring changes to the American health care system but all collapsed because of well-orchestrated attacks by conservative health economists, physicians, and insurance companies. While most Americans believe the government should make providing health insurance to all citizens a priority, employers in the United States are more concerned about the skyrocketing health insurance premiums and are demanding that the government focus on bringing down the health care costs. Who is to blame for not sharing the pain? While it's easy to blame this on Republicans' political game, citizens and employers should work toward finding a solution for affordable but quality health care for everyone. It would have been so much easier for the founding fathers to instill the universal health care in the country without the opposition from any unfavorable organizations or lobbyists that the presidents in the last hundred years have been fighting against.

Teddy Roosevelt was not only about reforming health care but also health in general, pressing Congress to pass the Pure Food and Drug Act and the Meat Inspection Act to maintain proper labeling of food and drugs and sanitary conditions at meatpacking plants respectively. He also worked to establish the U.S. Forest Service that created national parks, nature reserves, national forests, and national wildlife refuges, including the Grand Canyon and the Theodore Roosevelt National Park. Ideas were running galore for Teddy Roosevelt and without much resistance from competing lobbyists, he was able to initiate the construction of the Panama Canal, which helped to shorten the freight route between San Francisco and New York.

It is these exceptional ideologies of these great presidents that have made the United States what it is today; without them the United States wouldn't have been a superpower or a developed nation. It is the responsibility of the leader of the nation to make significant changes to the landscape of the country that he or she loves and leads; these changes are often noted and followed, by other nations who aspire to be as great as other great men and women. The leaders of the developing world who usually do not have the instincts of the great leaders of the developed world should take note and at least strive to instill this great mindset among them. While the founding fathers and early presidents of the United States created a firm foundation for the government and its economy, the latter presidents, like Franklin Roosevelt, introduced a number of programs that have become the backbone of the country's financial system. As the country evolved into a capitalist economy, Roosevelt, also known as FDR, became the central figure of twentieth-century U.S. government, taking care of the citizens during the Great Depression and World War II. While he devised the Social Security System to ensure economic security for the elderly, poor, and infirm, he also set up a number of government agencies to ensure the security of the working class during those hard times. Prominent among the agencies are Federal Deposit Insurance Commission (FDIC) that guarantees the safety of people's deposits in member banks, the Tennessee Valley Authority (TVA) that was started to build dams, power stations, modernize agriculture, and home conditions in the economically affected Tennessee Valley during the depression era, and most importantly, the Securities and Exchange Commission (SEC) that regulates (or during these days we should say *tries* to regulate) the Wall Street. Similar to the Obama stimulus package intended to spur the economy during bad times, FDR spent over $3 billion through the Public Works Administration that set up a national relief agency providing employment to over two million people during the depression.

While there are a number of U.S. presidents who are ranked at the bottom of the bucket, many of the great presidents have served as a model with a good balance of idealistic and realistic domestic and foreign policies that have set a high example for democracy, progressiveness, and liberalism throughout the world. The developing countries have taken bits and pieces of these examples to create their own version, but the bars have not been set high enough to achieve extraordinary results. The underdeveloped countries don't want to set a bar for their countries because they know they will fail miserably for lack of their own efforts. Even after centuries of British rule, the Indian government and the country have been utterly chaotic in a nonviolent way, and the country has managed to barely make its way into the sect of emerging markets thanks to its organized businesses and hard-working middle class. Every country has the collective ability to be an exceptional nation only if they don't lose their drive due to circumstances.

While achievements of the leaders of the developed and developing countries have been positive but on different levels, the dictators of the underdeveloped countries of Cuba and North Korea have involved themselves in heinous crimes against their people for no reason other than a high level of sickness. Over the past five or so decades, hundreds of thousands of people have been executed in Cuba by Fidel Castro's firing squad; many of the powerful men who helped Castro gain power are among the executed. This psycho monster was so insecure that he killed people who disagreed with him, disobeyed his orders, or who he perceived as a threat to his existence. Talking to foreigners was grounds for questioning their loyalty. This Charles Manson-like behavior by the Castro brothers may have given them a huge cult-like following but it also created a nightmare among people because of his terror that stretched from countries in Latin America to Africa. This dictatorial regime abused human rights on such a scale that the citizens did not feel they lived in a civilized society but in a poverty-stricken, lawless regime where citizens caught trying to leave the country without government approval were sent to prison framed as criminals. His uncivilized attitude extended to the point where citizens who were tested positive for HIV/AIDS or were suspected to be homosexuals or transsexuals were imprisoned and treated worse than a criminal. The extreme cruelties of this moronic dictator who is not worthy of being a leader of a country, many of the citizens of this hopeless country attempt to escape. This fool of a dictator was so out of his mind that he begged the Soviet Union to launch nuclear missiles on various U.S. cities in response to the U.S. economic embargo on Cuba.

Although Cuba may boast universal health care, it comes at the cost of the doctor's salary, which is set at about $20 per month. Services of the Cuban doctors are also provided in other countries and in return the dictatorial regime receives a large amount of subsidized commodities. In his quest to keep a firm grip on this once fabulous nation, the thug Castro got a law degree to bring lawlessness in the island and burn the country to ground with economic disaster, while he built his personal fortune (now in the hundreds of millions of dollars).

Similar to Cuba, the dictatorial regime in North Korea provides universal health care that is in name only, as more than half of the children in the country suffer from malnutrition and over 10 percent of the population has died from starvation in the past decade. This is despite massive food and other aid from the UN. The five-foot three-inch of a joker Kim Jong Il and his minions run a number of dreadful political prison death camps in the remote areas of the country for alleged enemies of the state and the politically unreliable. This ruthless regime that is mostly made up of extremely below average scum of the earth still believes in running torturous concentration camps populated with hundreds of thousands of people who are considered to encompass ideologies that are poisonous. The buffoon and his regime not only accused the concentration camp population of poisonous ideologies but also experimented with poisonous gas and biological toxins on those innocent civilians.

Because these two dictators who are extremely low in self-respect and extremely high in insecurity are getting away with so many crimes, including the destruction of their countries, there are many others who want to copy them. It is time the international community stands against their brutalities. While most of the people in the civilized world are deeply disturbed by the atrocities of these terrible dictators, there are a few want to-be dictators who sympathize with these regimes. Not only are the people from the rest of the world concerned, but also people in these countries are crying for help—not for meaningless food or other economic aid but help to relieve the dictators' death grips from the necks of these poor souls. These despicable autocratic dictators may feel good when they are being praised and saluted by hundreds of thousands of citizens who are often forced to do it, but they should know that everyone of them would kill the dictators without a blink if given a chance. These tyrannical leaders should stop holding public appearances because the rest of the world doesn't give a damn about them and only wish them death. It is in favor of these authoritarians that they don't show their face to the rest of the world since their faces are as ugly as their personalities, attitudes, and achievements. The next time people see these dictators out in public, they should hurl tomatoes or potatoes, especially rotten ones, at them to show what the public thinks of them. Students whose careers are at stake because of these dictators should challenge these incapable leaders by creating diplomatic relations with other student bodies all over the world and nonviolently revolting as a combined group. It is true that while most of the leaders of the developed world are above average in their leadership skills, most of the leaders of the developing world are average in their leadership skills. Quite in contrast are the leaders of the underdeveloped and dictators who are despicably below average in their leadership skills whose priorities are power and control at the cost of the country's economic destruction. The extreme behaviors of the societies in these worlds mostly follow their leaders in that it varies from above average to below average. While a quirky behavior in a developed world could be about finding extraterrestrial intelligence, that of an underdeveloped world could be to spread hatred among their people to kill other human beings.

In the middle of the leadership spectrum is an amazing story of Lee Kuan Yew, the former prime minister of Singapore, who turned the country around from a volatile, underdeveloped colonial outpost to a developed Asian Tiger. Even though the government maintained tight control of the economy, it offered attractive tax incentives for foreign investors to grow the economy. It is a lesson to be learned by the underdeveloped and developing countries that leaderships with creative and effective ideas can turn the conditions of a country around regardless of the circumstances. Yew did not just put ideas into practice; to be effective, he had to change the mindset of a number of corrupt individuals to make this transformation. Once these thorny situations were cleared, Yew successfully built modern infrastructure, affordable public housing, and promoted tourism. He was the kind of leader who didn't let his leadership go to his head, even though he was the sole decision maker for over three decades. This is something most underdeveloped and developing country leaders are not able to do because once they rise to that special seat, they realize the power they have and start taking undue advantage of their position, giving way to corruption, which slows down growth.

The U.S. military force maybe one of the largest and strongest in the world, but it has not been able to get the job completed in a number of instances because of a variety of reasons. While a number of developing countries are gaining nuclear weapon capabilities just to show off their so-called "power" to the rest of the world, the United States is working with the UN to make this a nuclear weapon free world, so that some mad and deranged leader won't be able to use that power. The total U.S. military spending currently is over $500 billion a year (excluding the operations in Afghanistan and Iraq) and is the largest in the world, with the bulk of the spending going toward operations/maintenance and more than 15 percent toward research/development. The total military budget of the Indian government is a little over $32 billion. The difference in military spending between the United States and India is mainly due to the fact that the United States has military bases in a number of countries all over the world and performs a lot more defense research than any other developed or developing country. One has to agree with the experts that U.S. military spending is way too excessive, as its military spending is almost the same as the rest of the world put together. One way to cut down on the military spending is to change the country's aggressive foreign policy, including the war on terrorism on which it has spent over $850 billion in Afghanistan and Iraq. Even excluding the spending on the war on terrorism, the United States could cut its military spending by a fifth and still fight any enemy or war that may come its way and provide internal security. U.S. military spending is a staggering ten times more than its cold war competitor and these overwhelming figures are not only due to the superpower's overly cautious measures but also to its overaggressive defense lobbyists who over a period of time have used the government's paranoia about the country's safety and security to their undue advantage.

The U.S. government needs to bring down its defense budget significantly and keep only programs that will secure the nation and its international treasures. One way to bring down the astounding defense budget is to reduce the number of international military bases it is currently operating. This could be done without compromising its hold on international security by creating strategic military partnerships with its allies. The other way is to cut down the amount and number of varieties of weapons built for the nation's military while increasing the selling of weapons to its allies without creating a weapons race or regional instability.

The Department of Homeland Security has the daunting task of protecting the country within against any terror attacks, protecting the borders, and responding to any natural disaster. They make these tasks seem easy with the help of the two powerful agencies namely the Federal Bureau of Investigations (FBI) and the Central Intelligence Agency (CIA) that are the most feared by national and international criminals. It is amazing how the undercover agents infiltrate gangs and groups to gather intelligence and nab them—which is all done by the book—before they could harm anybody. It's better to spend additional money to be proactive than spend substantial amounts of money to react after the fact. These two intelligence groups and even the military use sophisticated unmanned aerial vehicles known as drones to spy on gangs and groups without detection. These vehicles have also been used to hit precise enemy targets on the ground where a manned mission would be at high risk. No one should care about their phone being tapped or being monitored on the World Wide Web as long as they are not involved in any suspicious terrorism activities since those listening to your phone calls or monitoring the Web don't give a damn what you are talking about as long as it does not involve you putting together a scheme against the country or people. People should stop complaining that increased security and targeted searches in the airports amount to profiling and an invasion of privacy. These activities may seem like invasions of privacy, they are all required for keeping the nation secure from the hands of the insane. Invasion of privacy is only an excuse for them, but the real reason is the added inconvenience caused to them due to these extra measures as their patience has already been running low. These people who were not used to change stopped complaining once they got used to the additional inconvenience.

What about surveillance through security cameras? Is that considered invasion of privacy? Citizens in the United States should take a breather because there are over four million security cameras installed on each and every street in the United Kingdom to make the lives of cops there easier against crime fighting. Even with those many security cameras, crimes have not gone down and UK cops are still having a hard time solving them. More controversial has been the close to three million (and counting) security cameras with face recognition software installed on the streets in China. There is the question that the communist country could be using these monitoring devices for something more than tracking criminals. Citizens in the developed world should take a double breather because the governments have not introduced a program to insert RFID chips into individuals to fight crimes. If paranoid and less-informed dictators found out that RFID chips could be inserted into humans to track their day-to-day living and what they really thought about their leaders, people in those countries are going to be in big trouble—if they're not already.

The Central Bureau of Investigation (CBI) in India is not as powerful as the FBI both politically and functionally, and its substandard crime investigations have major political and economic impact, as corruption cases, financial crimes, and terrorism crimes have been ineffective as it cracks under pressure. Since the CBI handles some high-profile cases, it has been rightfully criticized for its inaction and for miring itself by political influence. While the FBI conducts undercover operations itself and only uses civilian informants for gathering information, the CBI is not very effective in performing undercover operations, so most undercover operations these days are conducted by journalists who expose the crooks through the national media. Once the case is exposed to the public, the CBI takes the case into its jurisdiction; journalists have come to realize that going undercover and exposing it to the national audience is the best way to wake the CBI and bring the crooks to justice. CBI should be given autonomy so it can act independently and investigate crimes efficiently, but most of the crooks being investigated are politicians themselves.

The social regulations implemented by the U.S. government over private companies to achieve social goals involve ensuring health and safety and environmental preservation by enforcing workplace safety standards for employees and air/water/land regulations for the environment. A developing country like India has had a different agenda for its social regulations due to its exponentially growing population. This has not been an issue for most of the developed world, including the United States. One of the main social regulations implemented by the Indian government is population growth control and family planning policy; policy makers and think tanks believe population growth was one of the greatest hindrances to economic development. The population growth control in India has become a major issue while it is believed that unless all of the population makes a concentrated effort toward family planning, the population may not stabilize until the year 2060. Unlike China, India is a democratic nation and cannot force the population to have only two children per family. These half-hearted efforts to curb the population both by the government and the people have seriously undermined India's efforts to become a major economic power in the emerging markets. If the Indian government does not wake up immediately, the increasing population problem is going to eventually result in food shortage.

Although teen pregnancy is not an issue in India as it is in the United States, the issue is that married couples don't have a limit on the number of kids they want to have. People don't rise above the occasion to think about these problems as a country, but they rather leave all these "critical thinking" to somebody else so they can go about their daily mundane lives. A small portion of the population that does the critical thinking and puts it into action is offset by the majority of the population that does not. If an entire generation or two stopped having kids or maybe limited themselves to one kid, the Indian population future will at least stabilize a bit and if not, great troubles are lurking ahead for them. It is the responsibility of the government to plan and implement a corrective action program that will align India's future population with numbers that will bring stability. The population growth rate in the 1940s was about 1 percent, and in the 1950s, the government started family planning efforts. Although hospitals provided birth control information to patients, doctors did not aggressively educate patients or encourage the use of contraceptives. India has brought family planning awareness to the public by educating and providing support to the low-income population regarding sexual and reproductive health, including the dangers of sexually transmitted diseases like AIDS. The Indian government did almost everything by the book—introduced family planning education as part of the school curriculum and introduced policies to improve the standard of living of the poor—but they didn't achieve the expected results.

In developed countries, industrialization and improved standard of living came with decreased population growth rate, and it was believed that India could attain the same goal by improving the general welfare of the population, especially families living in rural areas. Despite government's effort to curb population growth, the growth rate in the 1980s shot up to 2 percent and the birth rate in 1992 was still at thirty per thousand, which was down from the 1960s but not close to the target number that was to be attained twenty years ago. The involvement of women has improved their status by allowing them to bring about transformation in their community and changing the inferior status of women that has been profoundly ingrained in the society. The other culture that has been hurting family planning is the strong preference for sons—sometimes two sons rather than daughters in rural and low-income families for economic reasons. One reason is that sons are expected to work with the families on the farm or other businesses and take care of the family during old age. The second reason is due to the dowry system, which provides that during a daughter's marriage, her parents are expected to pay the son-in-law's family money in return for taking care of their daughter. Since the son-in-law's family sets the dowry money, sometimes the bride's parents are not able to afford the amount and that results in emotional issues for the family. Helping the low-income families make informed choices is always going to be ineffective because of these families' lack of basic education. These strategic plans of helping make informed choices would only work if the government makes drastic changes to its current plans through which it provides huge amounts of incentives to families that have only one child. Incentives in terms of free education for the only child, food stamps or food subsidies to the entire family, free entertainment, and special privileges to the entire family will be very persuasive. Plans of helping make informed choices to families without any huge incentives would only fall on deaf ears. The government has a choice to make—either take responsibility for the population growth and implement effective corrective plans with huge incentives to curb the population or let future governments assume the burden of uncontrolled population growth. Without action now, future governments may be forced to resort to drastic, undemocratic plans to effectively run the country with stable economy.

There are a number of social issues that affect everyone whether in a developed country or a developing one but the core issues people battle on a day-to-day basis vary from country to country. While developed nations like the United States struggle with mostly advanced issues like gun control, euthanasia, death penalty, and global warming, developing nations like India are still tackling, some successfully some not so successfully, primitive issues like population control, child labor, corruption, and literacy. Every country has gone through the same social issue at some point, but the various strategic ways these issues are dealt with makes some linger for decades in some countries while it could linger for centuries in some other. Even though there are a lot of global warming debates and critical claims of it not being an issue, one should take the basic data of rising ocean level and melting glaciers into consideration and make the minimum changes in your life that will help reduce the warming affects. Do it for future generations if not for your generation; your great-great-grand kids will thank you for it. Let's not blame the climate changes on increased solar activity or say that the evidence for a relationship between hazardous emissions and climate changes is only circumstantial. A jury would find a defendant guilty with enough circumstantial evidence and making simple changes in your lifestyle will not only help save energy but will save you money in the long run. Although China is the biggest culprit, it is the responsibility of every nation to set up policies and infrastructure to control emissions. It is perhaps more the responsibility of developing nations than developed, as they usually don't hold their end of the bargain.

Euthanasia, where one ends one's life in a painless manner, has been a controversial issue for a number of years. Although a lot of countries in Europe and two states in the United States have legalized some forms of euthanasia, it's time for all the states in the United States to legalize it. A number of prolife activists argue against it, but they need to understand that if an individual is in a brain-dead state or going through excruciating pain due to medical conditions, he or she should be allowed to decide whether to fight it through or end it with professional assistance. If one is in a brain-dead state, the end should come either by the person's medical will or if one does not exist, then a majority vote by the family and guardians together. Although there have been a number of cases in which people have come back to active life after being in a brain-dead state for decades, it should be up to the person or the family to make the decision to keep him or her on life support. In India, some liberals call the doctor's work of assisting to end one's life as a good deed; some conservatives believe that the doctor who ends a patient's life takes on the remaining karma of that person—which doesn't bode well in a scientific world.

While the mostly progressive society in the United States is still fifty-fifty prolife and prochoice from the standpoint of debate on abortion, the conservative society in India indirectly accomplished this by strongly encouraging abstinence until marriage. In India, the subject of abortion isn't even casually debated during family dinner; in the United States and other developed countries abortion is a matter of serious debate, and a consideration for citizens before choosing how to vote in presidential elections. Every presidential debate is filled with prolife and prochoice arguments and questions. My take on this issue is that every woman should have the right to decide whether to keep or end another life growing in her own body—whether she was raped by a stranger or a family member. In the case of a minor, a family vote should decide what should be done.

One could say stem cell research and advancement could be claimed as the most significant innovation in the field of medicine. It offers cures for a number of diseases, including cancer, but religious humanists and prolife supporters are crying foul since the process involves destroying human embryos. This is completely different from actually killing a live human being. But researchers are not giving up and are looking at alternatives to stem cell research that won't use human embryos. While I surely agree with President Obama, who recently lifted the ban on federal funding for stem cell research, I have seen people in their twenties and thirties die of heart attacks while people in their sixties happily drinking alcohol even after suffering five or six heart attacks. This makes me believe that if it's your time to die, nobody can change that and extending your life using stem cells is only another way of reaching your fullest lifetime that has been handed down to you. Prolife champions should look into the fact that centuries ago people were dying from complication of the flu, and life expectancy was much lower than it is today. Stem cell research will only take us to the next level of increased life expectancy. That being said, people should still make informed decisions about eating healthily, exercising, and drinking alcohol in moderation while not depending too much on medications unless when required. I am sure that prolife campaigners in the next century or two would be happy to have backed stem cell research, as it would have far-reaching implications in the medical field.

On the other hand, the death penalty, where one is put to death by the country's judiciary, is fair only if the person is convicted for killing another human being in a gruesome manner. Although prolife backers and a number of antideath penalty organizations claim that a society has no right to take a murderer's life, backers and organizations should understand that it's inhuman only if one is punished for a petty crime by stoning to death as some countries currently do. Prolife backers and organizations along with the help of international humane society should aggressively protest countries that torture petty crime suspects or innocent rape victims to death instead of wasting time on governments that execute murder suspects by lethal injection or hanging after lengthy trials.

Another social issue that's been bugging the developed world, especially the United States, is the increasing trend of teen pregnancy rates. While teen pregnancy in a developing country like India is nonexistent to negligible due to its socially and religiously conservative culture, the developed world has this problem due to its free and hippie culture. Most of these teens are single mothers who end up dropping out of school and living paycheck to paycheck. Eradication of this problem is tied to education and the U.S. federal government spends about $200 million a year educating its teens about the disadvantages of having a child at an early age. Most teens usually have the motivation to go to college and have a great career, but they get caught up in the moment, have an unintended pregnancy, and are faced with the difficult decision of whether to keep the baby or not. Although human life is valuable even in embryonic stage, when it comes to teen pregnancy, they should put their education and career first without even thinking twice. Doctors and family members should clearly give abortion as their first choice, while stating other alternatives, including giving the child up for adoption. But foster kids have way too many issues, which leaves the first choice as the only choice.

Teen pregnancy is not the only reason kids drop out of school; the second reason is due to their addiction to drugs (hard drugs or prescription drugs), which can be deadly when overdosed. Teen alcohol and drug use costs the federal government hundreds of billions of dollars, and cutting the suppliers off and convicting them with harsher sentences can only stop these illegal activities. One of the most debated social issues in developed countries, especially in the United States, is the legalization and taxation of marijuana for medicinal and recreational purposes. Although I am all for legalizing and taxing marijuana, but it has to be done for the right purposes and all facts and questions must be taken into consideration. Critics who support legalizing marijuana say the potential economic benefits of regulating and taxing it would be substantial, but this is questionable since all of the recreational users of marijuana use cash to buy it and that is hard to track to report for taxation. The cost of marijuana on people in the United States in a year now runs in the hundreds of billions of dollars due to health care, lost productivity, and crime, which is going to significantly rise as the drug is legalized. With the current marijuana trade in the United States valued at a little over hundred billion dollars, lawmakers believe the federal government can bring in about $40 billion dollars plus significant savings in legal costs, but even if this number is accurate, the cost of using it in terms of health care, lost productivity, and crime far exceeds the potential tax it could bring in. Once the ban on marijuana is lifted, even though some people believe that consumption is going to decrease, it is going to be otherwise, and crime rate is going to increase significantly since more people want to smoke marijuana. If the ban is lifted, what is going to happen to all the drug cartels from Mexico who currently supply the bulk of marijuana used in the United States? Are they going to openly escalate the drug war in the United States against local legitimate marijuana dealers, so they can control as much turf as possible to increase their revenue in this highly lucrative business? Is legalizing it only going to give birth to more homegrown drug cartels and gangs that will continuously engage in battles to control as much territory as possible? These are some of the many questions that need to be taken into consideration for creating tight regulations around growing and supplying the drug in this country.

While marijuana maybe a perfect short-term way out of depression and anger, if one gets hooked on it, that would be the only thing they would be holding on to—destroying everything else in one's life. Jobs, homes, families, and lives are lost because some people can't control slipping from recreational to habitual use. Critics claim that the U.S. government should curb the demand for it from its citizens through education and training. While I agree that success rates with these methods are very low, the best way to cut back on the demand is by restraining its supply from both domestic and foreign sources. Instead of blaming the U.S. government and its citizens for this issue, critics should see the astronomical size of various programs to curb this menace, in terms of rehabilitation and also curbing the supply from Mexican drug cartels. Without these programs, the use of marijuana and other drugs would be over the roof. The United States has the highest marijuana consumption rate in the world because it's readily available, relatively cheap, and soothing and intoxicating but not addictive like other hard drugs.

The U.S. government should lift the ban on marijuana for couple of years to test legitimizing this wonderful drug; if all goes well, it should lift the ban for a long time.

Racial inequality and crimes is a global issue that has subsided a lot in the developed world but lingers in the developing world. Racial inequality existed in the United States a long time ago, and in the twentieth century, random acts of brutality are classified as racial by media hype and unwanted attention. Any person living in the United States or any developed country who are a transformation of a developing or an under-developed country, whether Mexican or Asian Indian or African American should stop complaining about how they are treated here because they know they have it so much better than what they would have in their native country. Why ask for compensation for what happened to your forefathers when you know you are much better off here as compared to your counterparts in your native country, where all is in chaos either due to the government or the people.

On the other hand, many religious developing countries are battling with a similar social stigma that is caste based instead of race and the only way to deal with this is to give equal opportunity to everybody regardless of their caste or race. The problem occurs when special privileges are given to upper caste or lower caste or a race; treating everybody equally in every part of the society will solve this problem over time if not overnight.

The Indian government has laid out plans to become energy independent by the year 2012 by using alternative energies like bio-fuel, solar and wind power. But to achieve this goal the government should aggressively provide subsidies to all its citizens who manufacture or use these alternative energies. The United States is heavily pushing itself into alternative energy sources, without compromising its environment, to become self-sufficient. It is India and other developing countries that need to aggressively push toward self-reliance by using alternative energy sources because of their poor environmental standards and huge population. If anybody thinks that God will change the design of the human body in future generations so people can adapt to a brutal environment as a result of this generation's irresponsible actions, they are completely wrong. There simply won't be many future generations if we all keep up our irresponsible actions that destroy the environment and fail to actively compensate for the damage. The only way to compensate and save future generations is to not damage and destroy now. The best way to accomplish this is to give the environmental policies equal importance with economic policies, so they become part and parcel of the government, businesses, and people. No hodge-podge rules and regulations are ever going to cut it, and the only way to be effective is by implementing the best rules and regulations that encourage public compliance.

The Indian government should encourage the use of bio-fuel by providing incentives not only to farmers and landowners who grow the plants but also to vehicle owners in terms of tax rebates for users of these alternative energy sources. The government should reach out to its people by advertising the advantages of manufacturing and using these alternative energies in order to successfully achieve its goal of becoming energy independent. To meet the electricity demand of the huge population, the government disconnects power to various parts of the cities and towns almost everyday, which affects the day-to-day operations of a number of businesses and results in a significant loss of revenue. Instead of shutting power off to meet the demand, the government needs to use solar and wind sources to create more electricity. The government needs to give subsidies and tax breaks for businesses to set up wind farms and homeowners who install and use solar power. Load shedding to meet demand is not a good strategy to grow an economy. For the alternative energy plan to be a success, the Indian government should walk the walk and not just talk the talk by taking aggressive action plans from the books of some already successful developed nations, The Indian government needs to understand that whatever they are currently doing for these programs is obviously not working—so always learn from the best. Unless the government aggressively promotes the value of these alternative energy sources and helps ease initial setup cost outlays, these energy plans are not going to be fruitful.

The Indian government should adopt a plan similar to Boone Pickens's plan in the United States but maybe on a smaller scale. This plan to rely on wind power to generate electricity would not only reduce dependence on foreign oil but also reduce carbon dioxide emissions. A number of homeowners in India are dependent on natural gas for their cooking needs, and these should be transformed to electricity, so that all domestically manufactured natural gas can be used to power vehicles. All governments should seriously consider shifting to maximum use of alternate energy sources that would reduce dependence on foreign oil and at the same time increase savings and reduce environmental damage.

While it may not be practical to shut down all coal-fired power plants both in developed and developing countries, realistic, short-term but quick approaches to reducing carbon dioxide emissions should be strictly enforced, even if it means providing subsidies and tax breaks to these businesses. This is especially true for developing countries, where these emissions have reached astronomical proportions. Governments should also not give permission for new coal-fired power plants unless they completely eliminate carbon dioxide emissions. The other byproduct of these power plants is the hundreds of millions of tons of toxic coal ash waste that contains mercury, lead, arsenic, and other toxins that could make you terminally sick if you are the unlucky one. Don't believe it if a coal industry lobbyist says that the coal ash is not toxic because they are lying. This is one of the main reasons we should get rid of coal-fired power plants in the long run and push for the alternative energy resources.

Another social issue that's been bugging India is the high number of illiterate citizens. It is hard to understand whether illiteracy leads to lack of motivation or illiteracy is due to lack of motivation, but the illiterate population in this most populous democracy is almost equivalent to the current population of the United States, which is an astronomical number. Even after two centuries of rule by the highly educated British, the literacy rate in India is a little over 60 percent, which is equal to the population over six decades ago when it gained independence from the British. Although the literacy rate in India is growing, it is slower than the rate of population growth, and the government should take aggressive steps to reverse the two growth rates that will significantly increase the human development index. The government should motivate Indian youths by showing them the advantages of getting into the workforce as a college graduate. That would increase the literacy rate and the per capita income. The corporate structure in developed countries usually motivates their unskilled labor force to earn degrees by paying for tuition while also ensuring a better future in the company; corporations in developing countries should incorporate similar policies to earn more points in social governance. This structure is not limited to huge corporations; smaller businesses usually provide vocational and management training to their employees. That helps employees get ahead in their career, which in turn helps increase a company's talent force.

Corporate social responsibility (CSR) is not about pushing a company's brand image in the public's face or marketing their products or creating more revenue for the company but about creating an image for itself by involvement in social causes like environment, education, etc. Corporations in developing countries need to be active in those areas and should take a note that CSR is not just about environment and education but also providing safe and humane working conditions for their employees, protecting workers' rights, and adhering to all child and forced labor criteria. CSR focused on employees is only a small portion of the entire social responsibility landscape as companies in developed nations contribute considerable amount of its pretax earnings to charities and stretch every revenue dollar to match employee volunteer hours in the community. It is extremely important for companies and businesses in developing and underdeveloped countries to take a leadership role by adhering to these standards. Less-informed companies will follow their steps. Corporations and businesses in these countries should be ranked according to their CSR efforts, and the media should praise the highly ranked companies while chastising poorly ranked but well-known, branded companies for their lack of CSR efforts. The ranking should clearly state which companies are lagging behind in what section of their CSR endeavors; this should trigger an awakening in the company's management that would dedicate more resources to turn it around. The most successful and profitable companies with high corporate social responsibility rankings are from developed countries; they shape their business models to address social issues in a sustainable way, and companies in developing countries also can attain long-term profitability by simply following these models. These kinds of corporate mindsets don't just come with being literate or having a college degree but by having uncanny dynamic ability to see things both at the macro and micro level that usually gets wired in one's brain. The governments in these developing countries don't have the mindset of a developed world, but they should at least have the responsibility to provide clear CSR guidelines for companies to follow and thereby help enrich the state of the country. While there are number of social issues that need to be debated and appropriately acted on, the importance and the tactics of action sometimes change based on certain events inside or outside a country.

Being a free country and one made of immigrants with dreams of reaching their full potential, the United States also offers asylum and refugee protection to individuals who show that their lives or freedom would be threatened if they returned to the country in question. This has been the policy of most developed and free countries that have an inherent belief in human rights. Even though they don't agree with the inhumane conduct of the dictator, communist, or the lawless rebels in the refugees' home country, in recent years these policies have been carefully reviewed because refugees could be here to destabilize national security. Although refugees with legitimate threat to their lives back in their country may get their application denied after a more careful review, these free countries with good intentions have every right to deny any application and safeguard the lives of the citizens of their country. Although critics may claim different reasons, including discrimination, for denial of these applications, the governments have the right to make sure they don't let any members of any terrorist organizations enter the country especially after the 9/11 tragedy. It's better to be a hard ass and refuse all these questionable refugee applications than to regret the decisions later because you allowed these questionable characters with ulterior motives inside the country.

Presidents of democratic countries have the responsibility of picking a justice for the Supreme Court who not only has political and ideological views in line with the president, but also in line with current Supreme Court judges. That creates a balanced group and unbiased outcomes for all issues appearing before the court. Presidents of the developed world and the legislative bodies that approve the selection of the supreme court justices go through months of crucial review of all the candidates, checking their backgrounds, qualifications, experience, and most importantly, how they would fit into the existing panel of justices. It is true that presidents in the developing world select a supreme court judge who has the most experience and not necessarily to create a balanced group mainly because the issues that come up in front of the highest court in developing countries are not political or ideological. One won't see a case like Terri Schiavo in front of any higher court in a developing country, where politicians or advocacy groups won't get themselves involved in prolife movements or pro-disability rights movements because they don't exist. In a conservative, developing country like India, the husband has the higher authority to make decisions about his wife's life and death if she is in a persistent vegetative state. Parents lose their rights to their daughters once the daughters marry. The slowly conservative-to-modern transforming Indian society still would not have given so much media attention to a similar case, which would have been quickly closed because it would be the right of the husband more than the parents to decide the wife's fate of life and death.

The U.S. government, with the help of Food and Drug Administration (FDA), has been on top of implementing standards/regulations on food products and medical drugs. This is not true in India, where the Director General of Health Services (DGHS) has that function. The DGHS is not as powerful as FDA due to rampant corruption. A DGHS official can easily be bribed by the offender to cover up any issue or problem, which doesn't help improve the quality of service in the food industry. It is not enough for the central leadership to be strong and powerful—each and every wing under the government must be powerful enough to create, implement, and enforce effective laws. While food regulations do exist in India, it's really easy to sweep violations under the rug. The FDA not only powerfully regulates human food but also food intended for animals. When FDA inspectors find contamination in human or animal food, the product is recalled and withdrawn from the market. The FDA continues working until the root cause of the contamination is found and eliminated. Inspectors also perform regular tests in restaurants, and each restaurant gets a score based on the quality, safety of the food handling, and cleanliness of the place. All scores are put on Web sites for the public to view and make informed choices. Even after these tight regulations and enforcement, there are an estimated 76 million illnesses, over 300,000 hospitalizations, and about 5,000 deaths in the United States due to food-borne illness, which is considerably lower than in any country in the developing world.

As far as pets are concerned, none of them can be neglected or taken care of poorly in the developed world because the owners are booked for criminal conduct by the Society for Prevention of Cruelty to Animals (SPCA). One can see thousands of stray, neglected pets wandering the cities of developing countries. The governments in developing countries are not smart and fast enough to keep up with all the important everyday issues, and it makes one mad because they have the time to indulge in many corrupt practices.

Developing countries need to use and enforce similar models. The food analysts and inspectors in India are less concerned about the public's health and safety, and they collaborate with offenders to provide inferior products and services to generate profit for themselves. As always, there are exceptions to the rule, but the vast majority who engage in these unsafe activities with no regard to the public's welfare surpasses them. In a developing country like India, corruption, huge population, and economic conditions overrule these standards and regulations. Street vendors and open market vendors, usually run by low-income families, would lose their livelihood if shutdown because of lack of hygiene and quality standards. So the street vendors who are usually illiterate and do not understand the food regulations pay bribes to the food inspector for allowing them to skirt the safety and quality standards and to the cops to let them run a mobile shop on the side of the street illegally. Vendors blame the officials for forcing them to use bribes and the officials blame the vendors for begging them not to enforce regulations. The finger should be clearly pointed toward the officials, as they are the ones not enforcing the regulations and endangering the public. The vendors in the open market may be operating legally but are usually paying the food inspectors.

If the DGHS were to shutdown all these street vendors for not keeping up to the health and safety standards, the economy of the country would be in chaos as the majority of these street vendors' livelihood is from their vending. On the other hand, the DGHS could easily enforce the health and safety regulations on these street vendors and make sure they stick to it. One way for the DGHS to make sure the street vendors stick to the regulations is by displaying the test score for quality, safety of the food handling, and cleanliness of the place in front of the street vendor's stall. Then the public could make informed choices before buying. Street vendors who fail the quality and safety standards test should be given a chance to improve their standards through free education and training. Repeat offenders should be given a final warning before they are required to shutdown their operation. Packaged products provide lists of ingredients, but products purchased on the street lack ingredient lists and expiration dates. It is not just the flies on the sweets that are a concern but also the color additives in products. Usually officials are slow to react on any issues of adulteration without public or media outcry forces a ban. When a vendor sells illegal but not harmful adulterated food like watered milk, officials are lethargic and ignorant in their response even after public and media outcry.

If the government and people don't make incremental changes, it would be no surprise that there will be generations spent without any social progress. Well-informed consumers who are aware of the health hazards and the laws protecting them can solve the issue of food adulteration. In India, there are about eight million mom and pop stores selling food commodities and products that don't maintain any health regulations and quality standards; as India moves toward more streamlined food processing and larger businesses that are attentive to food regulations, these issues can be resolved. Instead of waiting for the larger businesses to start operating with concern for food regulations standards, the DGHS should also extend the quality standards test score for public display for the eight or so million mom and pop stores selling food. Failure to comply with the regulations should result in a final warning followed by shutting down the store. Another way the government and the DGHS can force higher food safety and quality standards on these mom and pop stores is by approving more and more multinational food corporations who already maintain significantly higher safety and quality standards than their Indian counterparts. Although in a developing country like India one cannot totally avoid the mom and pop stores or open market and street vendors, safety precautions can be taken to weed out the unsafe. One can check the general cleanliness of the cook; cleanliness of the area including flies, insects, and rodents; water source for the food; and storage of uncooked food; All these general checks must be initiated and test scores displayed in front of these businesses.

While the developing world grapples with the issue of inferior and badly contaminated food products, the developed world is struggling with a sophisticated social issue of eating organic or non-organic foods. Since the yield of organic food products is a little less than the non-organic food products, the cost of organic products is a little higher, but the advantage of consuming organic products are their significantly higher antioxidant levels. It is very important for consumers to make adjustments to eat organic food products more and more as antioxidants help fight cancer. If consumers can't afford to buy organic for everyday consumption, they should at least alternate between organic and non-organic every time they go to the grocery store. Organic food products producers and grocery stores on the other hand should increase the production and marketing of organic products so consumers are more aware of the advantages. Both producers and consumers should create a balance between increasing profit and delivering and consuming healthier food products. Restaurants, including fast food places, should adopt organic products on their menu and advertise the advantages on the menu itself so people are very aware of them. The federal and state governments should step in and provide subsidies to farmers to grow more organic fruits, vegetables, and meat products. As more consumers eat organic, they get healthier and the government in turn will be spending less on health care costs for the elderly. On the contrary, in developing countries like India where agriculture has mainly been organic with low yields, there has been a huge drive to go non-organic to increase the yield and profits, but farmers should be taught about the harmful effects of non-organic food products. It is extremely important to have a balance of organic and non-organic food products so the farmers are able to increase their yields and profits, and consumers are able to eat healthier. Governments should definitely step in to provide subsidies to farmers to not convert all their harvests to non-organic and educate the farmers and consumers of the importance of organic food products.

The FDA also regulates prescription drug advertising and promotion to ensure companies are advertising the specific medical purpose for which the drug was approved and that the advertisement contains both the benefits and risks of the drug. The FDA also recently started conducting quality-control inspections of low cost drugs and drug ingredients in manufacturing plants in India and China, major suppliers to the U.S. generic and over-the-counter market. After an approved drug makes it to the market, the FDA remains alert for any adverse effects. If there are too many side effects on many patients, the FDA has the right to pull the drug off the market. The food and drug regulation came into effect in the early twentieth century when Harvey Wiley, then chief chemist at the Department of Agriculture, conducted research on the adulteration and misbranding of food and drugs on the American market. Over the following decades the FDA has evolved into a strong and powerful authority on food and drugs, yet it only gets involved after an issue has hit the mass media, which is a little late given that critical and complicated commodities like food and drugs are involved. On the other hand, once it gets involved, the FDA makes quick resolutions to issues so no further damage is done to the public.

Continuous improvements to regulations are a norm, and in 2006 a committee of experts found deficiencies in the FDA approval system and called for further regulatory powers, funding, and independence for the FDA. These kinds of continuous improvements and independence are required for all regulatory authorities in developing countries. Indian pharmaceutical industry has been growing tremendously because of increased demand for low cost generic and over-the-counter drugs, and in 2007, total pharmaceutical exports from India stood at $5.5 billion. The United States is India's largest overseas market, but the recession has forced American companies to cut prices on generic drugs by as much as 65 percent, resulting in a pharmaceutical export growth rate of just 7 percent. In the beginning of the twentieth century, domestic drug industry was nonexistent in India, and all drugs were imported. This changed after the First World War. Domestic and foreign pharmaceutical companies started producing drugs in India to compete with imported drugs. To check the quality of these drugs, the government, under British rule, started a regulating authority. Changes to regulations for food and drugs have been implemented slowly and steadily in India, but the most dramatic change that is going to drive the cost of generic drugs high is the new patent regulation. The new WTO rules on intellectual property are not only going to affect the poor in developing countries but also a number of uninsured in the developed world. The drug industry influence to keep drug cost high will eventually reach a point where nobody will be able to afford drugs, resulting in unspeakable consequences to people. Similar to the rifle association in the United States, the drug association just doesn't give a damn, but there will be a time when they have to set aside their arrogance and give a damn about human beings not just profits.

In a decade, U.S. demand for low-cost generic drugs from Indian pharmaceutical companies had increased by forty times, resulting in loss of market share for non-generic drug makers. This resulted in the formation of the Bulk Pharmaceuticals Task Force (BPTF), which represents the American makers of drug ingredients who believe the risk to human health from these generic drugs from India and China is increasing exponentially. The increase in demand is mainly due to baby boomers who have been ill and travel to Canada and Mexico to buy low-cost generic and over-the-counter drugs. Instead of criticizing the quality of generic drugs from India and China, the U.S. drug industry should collaborate with them to create a win-win situation for both. The FDA does not approve of Americans buying cheap generic prescription medications from other nations; there should be awareness that all citizens cannot afford the high cost of medications in the United States and the rules should be relaxed. Instead the agency turns a blind eye to the problem and the foreign drugs. The FDA says these prescription medications can be brought home if they consumable only for ninety days. While U.S. drug companies have their head up their ass, the FDA is showing common-sense toward the health requirements of the baby boomers.

One may wonder why for prescription medications in the United States are so expensive, and the answer is the high cost of bringing drugs to market, including research and development, testing, etc. It can cost as much as $1 billion to bring a new drug to market, and not all drugs that go through the process pass FDA testing standards. Then one may ask is Why don't the drug manufacturers make generic versions of the drugs?" Well, they didn't initially since they were happy selling their high-cost non-generic drugs, but once the generic drugs from other countries started flowing into the United States, the drug manufacturers had no alternative but to create their own version of the generic drugs to compete.

Although all of Europe and a number of developing countries, including India and Thailand, have some form of universal health care, the U.S. government has shunned universal health care. President Obama has assured his people that he will bring real change by introducing affordable and accessible health insurance to all citizens. Everybody has their fingers crossed, but we will have to wait and see how much of his promise he is going to deliver.

Health care critics like Bill Maher believe that the main cause of illness in the United States is the poor diet of its citizens and lowering the cost of medication is only a superficial change in health care system. While I agree that poor nutrition is the main reason for obesity and a number of diseases, changing the way people eat and enforcing regulations on the way food products are grown is a long-term process. Therefore I agree with the president's first step in reducing health insurance costs. Even if one is eating a healthy diet, that person is still paying a huge health insurance premium because good nutrition does not mean an end to illness. Some hereditary illnesses, for example, aren't tied to diet. The government can't force people to not eat at fast food chains or restrict them to only one greasy meal a day, but it should initiate an overhaul of the food industry and provide tighter regulations that will help citizens eat a healthier diet. On the other hand, advocates of pure capitalism oppose any kind of universal health care since that is totally going to bring down the profit-driven health care industry. Republican politicians and their money-hungry health care lobbyists oppose universal health care because it would mean lower share prices that in turn results in significantly lower bonuses to the executives of health care organizations. That leaves lobbyists missing their cut and politicians losing political campaign contributions.

Not all media personalities are for a universal healthcare system as talk-radio host Rush Limbaugh does not want the federal government to take over healthcare with the public option because he believes he will lose his prescription painkillers that he is so addicted to. We would rather have Limbaugh blabber uncontrollably in the comfort of his studio about unregulated free-market capitalism than get into the political landscape because he will drop out of the scene miserably worse than he flunked out of college. Hypothetically speaking, if Limbaugh were president, all corporate executives involved in scandals would have escaped prosecution in the name of unregulated capitalism. Instead of challenging Obama on a debate, Limbaugh should coax all ex corporate executives spending time in prison to be his pen pals so they can talk about unregulated capitalistic ideologies in their love letters.

Why not provide a government-run public health care insurance option to citizens, including the millions of uninsured Americans, so they are not left to die if they encounter a deadly disease? This will also make the health care insurance industry more competitive. Contrary to popular belief, the private health care industry will not eventually go bankrupt; instead this will lead to mergers and acquisitions that will help the big private health care organizations. The biggest health care insurance scam of the century would be the one in which uninsured citizens would be fined for not having insurance. It is utterly shameful that the politicians are giving in to the crocodile tears of health care insurance lobbyists and ruining it in the name of the free-market system.

The health care insurance companies are denying the legitimate claims by patients left and right for the sake of profits. The health care insurance industry in the United States should be overhauled both in terms of cost and service, and put in line with its counterparts in Europe. Doctors in the United States have become like auto mechanics that recommend unnecessary, expensive surgeries over cheaper and more effective alternatives, so they can milk their patients of the health insurance money. Its not just unnecessary, expensive surgeries but also too many CT scans and MRIs, which are easy and quick and big money makers. Some dirty doctors have ordered way too many of these scans for their patients, and that has resulted in unnecessary tests as much as 35 percent all over the country. These dirty doctors are not only milking the insurance money but also putting the lives of their patients at risk with increased exposure to radiation. Patients should be proactive by asking the doctors tough questions regarding the number of tests, and if patients suspect tests are unnecessary, they should post a detailed description of these dirty doctors online for the benefit of other patients. Just because a doctor has a huge student loan to payoff doesn't mean he or she gets to put the patients' life at risk. As the renowned personal finance expert Suze Orman says, doctors should remember that people come first and then comes money. Just like its hard and rare to find an honest auto mechanic who won't screw you with unnecessary work on your vehicle, its hard and rare to find a doctor who you can trust with your body—true but sad story.

Since health care is such a sensitive subject for the public, the U.S. government should bring health care reforms, piece by piece, to the table explaining and advertising each to the public with the help of numbers. Ridiculous outbursts by people in town hall meetings during health care debates show that they are not only ignorant but also hesitant to change, and they would rather see no action than accommodate changes to make things better. Often the real advantages of reforms get entangled in politics, but if the advantages are explained in numbers to the public, the political cloud can be easily cleared. It is really sad that Ted Kennedy, a life-long advocate of health care overhaul, didn't get to see health care reforms during his lifetime. When significant health care changes are made in this country, Ted's brave soul is going to rest in peace; it is the responsibility of the American public to give that to him.

Extending CSR to the government doesn't mean that the government should be run like a corporation or that it should blindly throw some money away to the community to show how caring it is to the people. Before taking care of the community, a safety net should be laid to take care of its employees. If an employer can't take care of its employees at workplace to make sure they can perform to the best of their abilities in perfect health, how can they take care of the community? This is where the government steps in to enforce workplace safety and health standards to prevent work-related injuries, illnesses, and deaths both in public and private sector workplaces. This is very true in developed countries, but for the approximately 400 million combined Indian workforces in the agriculture, industry, and services sectors, only a handful of the large companies offer a comprehensive occupational health and safety standards. Even trade unions in India and other developing and underdeveloped countries have a very limited role in occupational health and safety due to their lack of knowledge of the existence of these standards. In other words, occupational health safety is still in its infancy in India, and the best way for trade unions and employees to stand up to these issues is to hire a lawyer who specializes in workplace safety issues. Standing up to these issues with the help of an expert is the only way the government and the employers are going to address these problems. In 2002, about 50,000 occupation-related fatal injuries were reported in India, which is significantly higher than in any developed country and alarming for a country that is on the road to economic boom.

India has realized that for it to be one of the Asian economic power-houses it needs to build the entire package, with all-inclusive amenities. It's not enough for it to just sit on a good education system that was mostly done by the British during their rule. Implementation of comprehensive occupational health and safety standards must be part of that fully loaded package or the economic boom will come to a standstill after reaching a saturation point. It needs to realize that it cannot expect the economy to grow continuously even if it continues to allow multinational corporations into the country to take advantage of the output of the good education system. It must build a broad action plan that includes the effective implementation of occupational health and safety standards. The two most common work-related injuries in the United States are either due to personal neglect or are unavoidable. In India common work-related injuries are mainly due to an employer's neglect and lack of knowledge of safety standards. Injuries can also be blamed on lack of enforcement of safety standards by the government, so it's important for employees and lawyers to take the initiative to fight the causes and hold the employers and the government accountable. The Indian government blames the lack of action plans on a decentralized system of occupational health safety standards whereby the regulations are set by the central government and the local governments carry out the implementation using funding from the WHO and ILO. Then why don't they change the organizational structure to make it work? This blame game by governments in developing and underdeveloped countries can be reduced when people educate themselves on their rights.

Child labor is another sensitive workplace issue that is rampant in India and other developing countries because the employer benefits from cheap labor and the underage employee's wages help to feed his or her low-income family. The employee is a kid who could easily range in age from five- to fifteen-years-old, and the problem doubles when they are working in extremely unsanitary conditions. The governments have been working on various proactive measures to tackle this huge socioeconomic child labor problem that flourishes because of the poverty and illiteracy in most developing countries. In India, a committee was formed to study the cause and effect of child labor, and the committee found it impractical to completely ban it because of the link to poverty. It chose to ban child labor in certain areas and regulate the conditions of work in other areas. This enforcement rule has completely fallen on deaf years, resulting in total inaction from the governments. Kids under the age of fifteen should be completely banned from working in developing and underdeveloped countries and allowed to go to school. Governments should come up with alternative ways for low-income parents to pick up the tab by increasing the minimum wage and providing food stamps. In developed countries, teenagers start working part time while attending school but never under hazardous conditions. Kids who get to work in the real world as teens are better prepared for their career and life's responsibilities. A lot of teens work in developed countries (but not in hazardous conditions) to either save for college or spend it while they get some real-world experience that may or may not come handy later on in life.

A loose analogy for the child labor problem in developing countries would be the illegal immigration problem in the United States and most other developed countries. In the United States, there are millions of illegal immigrants that have come from all over the world but mainly from Mexico. There are mainly two reasons why the U.S. government is focused on tracking and deporting illegal immigrants: one is that these illegal immigrants are fleeing poor economic conditions and save money to send it to their families, and the second is that these people form the backbone of the U.S. agriculture and other low-paying employment community. Parents who send their young kids to work in India have a mindset that extra cash in their pocket will help provide three meals a day for the large family. This mindset is not exclusive to India but is evident in most of the developing and underdeveloped nations. A number of multinational corporations from developed nations have been bashed by human rights organizations for using children to work in factories under hazardous conditions in developing countries.

The world has been growing at a rapid rate and soon the adverse effects of growth were visible in the environment that affected the human health. The developed minds have recognized the problem and have initiated ways to protect human health. They have started programs to reduce the damage to air, water, and land; whereas developing minds are still completely in denial of the environmental effects. Just like any of their other programs, the developing minds are haphazardly putting together environmental programs that they know just won't work. Currently in the United States, the air quality in a lot of cities is below EPA standards and is hazardous for humans. The government is making renewed efforts to clean up smog, but compared to air quality in developing countries, the developed world has much cleaner air because of better enforcement of standards. In India, this could be due to a lack of regulation during the British rule and poorly regulated environment later, compounded by the overloaded population and an economically booming, emerging market. They just can't keep expecting the economic surge to take care of everything else. Just like in the United States, state governments should take initiatives to regulate emission standards wherever federal government oversight is lacking. The combined approach should make for an effective campaign against all emissions.

The 1980s saw a population growth rate of 2 percent in India and deforestation for cultivation of cash crops, plantation crops, horticulture, and use of timber and forestland for other purposes. This forced the government to create regulations that enabled the protection and conservation of forests, and illegal deforestation became punishable with penalties and imprisonment. But what is the point of these regulations if the culprits can get away by paying bribes to government officials?

With many cities smothered by smog because of traffic and industrial waste, it is time to put aggressive action plans in place. The mindset of the developing governments should change because they just react with a verbal promise when there is media or public outcry and later fade away. The standards put together by the central governments of these developing and underdeveloped countries are easily nullified by the hand-in-hand adulteration and fixing actions of local governments and businesses. The central governments may incorporate environmental considerations into their development programs, but the local governments and businesses feel these added regulations are only in place to curb economic growth. Unless this one-track mindset of economic growth without addressing safety and environmental issues is changed, it will cost them big time later. There are over fifty million registered motor vehicles in India and hundreds of thousands of factories polluting the air, water, and land, but the government and the people are only interested in economic growth. If there is no resolution among people and businesses to put a check on environmental pollution and an immediate tough stand from the government to crack down on culprits, it's going to be a lot harder to clean up the mess later. In the United States, there are activists and government agencies that keep these issues in check. There is also a huge push for going green by using organic products, driving hybrid vehicles, and using solar and wind energy. People should take it one step further and ride bicycles or Segways for short commutes; that will make the environment greener. Using an automobile for a five- or ten-minute commute is not good for the engine and riding bicycles or segways would not only extend the engine life but also save on gas and minimize pollution.

Then there are activists like former vice president Al Gore who worked on a documentary and wrote a book in 2006 called *The Inconvenient Truth* about global warming. For the movie's efforts to educate the public about the harmful effects of global warming and push for more government action to regulate, it won an Academy Award, along with other international awards. There are a lot of skeptics all around the world doubting the science behind global warming data presented in the documentary. Most scientists agree that global warming is occurring all around the world, but most lack the data to understand its effects and scale. The environmental documentary *Arctic Tale* showed deep and direct environmental issues like global warming, pollution, and most importantly, shrinking arctic ice. The documentary *The 11th Hour* explains how frequent and extreme hurricanes, earthquakes, and other natural disasters are the result of negative climate and environmental changes.

There have been a number of documentaries made about the environmental issues in India, but none have been able to make an impact on society mostly due to people's indifference to these issues. In the United States people spend considerable time to learning ways to change their lifestyle to positively impact the environment. Documentaries in developing countries should be made more interesting and controversial to attract the attention of common people and educate them about the alternatives. Most of the people in developing countries have the narrow-minded mentality that if anything does not affect their or their family's day-to-day life, it doesn't concern them. They cannot or do not want to think beyond their everyday life and have a mentality that they would rather watch an entertaining movie rather than wasting money on an informative documentary.

With the housing and banking system collapse in 2008, the U.S. government is looking to spend more to create jobs in wake of the high unemployment rate. In addition to that, the $750 billion stimulus package for various sectors, including the auto industry will let the economy keep afloat until it recovers. All taxpayers may agree with the stimulus package, but most would disagree about the millions of dollars from the bailout money paid as bonuses to executives of troubled companies. These companies' executives think that it's okay to spend the bailout money on bonus checks even though the company is not making any profit because they at some point had given campaign contributions through their lobbyists. The strange politician-lobbyist bedfellow relationship should stop and so should giving unwarranted bonuses to executives. Why would any business and their head honchos in their sane mind give out millions of dollars of taxpayer money to their executives when their business is struggling? Is it just human nature that one wouldn't have any guilty feeling if they were to squander somebody else's money? Would any normal person do that and still sleep well at night? Are these company executives so greedy that they wouldn't feel any remorse for taking taxpayer money even when the company and the country are in a dire financial mess? The government needs to step in at this critical time and put down rules as to how the bailout money could not be used by companies—especially on executive pay. Although the government has said that it cannot control how companies use the bailout money, it has the right to tell the companies how not to use it since it is taxpayers' hard-earned money.

The government did cap the CEO pay to $500 thousand, but more needs to be done in terms of putting caps on bonuses to executives and even employees during tough economic times. It is alarming to see that the executives think that they are entitled to bonuses even when the company has suffered significant losses or gone under. When the insurance giant AIG got over $150 billion in bailout money, the first thing its board of directors did was to put $600 million into a bonus fund to pay the executives. The first thing that comes to my mind is are you f***ing kidding me? It took the intervention of New York State Attorney General, a huge media outcry, and a $60 billion loss to suspend the bonus payments—afterward these shameless bastards, I mean executives, asked the government for more bailout money. Either the morons at AIG did not learn their lesson or their egos were too big, so they had to take bonuses from the bailout money even after a staggering loss reported by the company. Although a lot of taxpayers were angry, one has to also feel pity for these executives who are totally clueless of the big picture, and the U.S. government did the right thing by asking the bonuses to be given back to the taxpayer. The government needs to spend a little more time looking into these corporate giants' books to make sure they are using taxpayers' money wisely and that they really need the money to survive. With so much debt the government has accumulated and so much taxpayer money at stake, it is only wise for the government to step in and ensure the money is spent on the right companies and for the right reasons.

These moronic AIG executives and all other greedy Wall Street bastards who think of stealing taxpayer money need to understand that forty-seven of the American states are facing a budget deficit of $350 billion for the next two years. That will mean cuts to low-income family health insurance, education, and cuts to state workforces. All these greedy executives should be utterly ashamed of themselves for robbing American taxpayers in the name of company bonuses. If Bush were the president, there would have been no action from the government as far as AIG bonuses were concerned. On top of these bonuses, these crooks from AIG have been deliberately trying to ignore legitimate claims from a number of customers who have been injured in the war in Iraq, while the executives were enjoying expensive spa and golf retreats. It is only fair to see the frustrations of the American citizens have prompted hate mail and death threats against AIG employees. Maurice Greenberg who held the post of CEO at AIG for over thirty-five years is closely associated with the Republican Party and one of the reasons Bush jumped into bailing out the company before the end of his second term. This is exactly why lobbyists and powerful business friends should be kept out of Washington, so that screwing the general public is kept to zero or at least to a bare minimum. When the government has too many associations with lobbyists and business friends who are running around in the political inner-circle, it is too easy for the government to cross the line and give too many favors to friends and not many to the general public.

All the Republican politicians, including Mr. Jindal, who supported the spending on war in Iraq, should stop complaining about the bailout package since this will help strengthen the U.S. economy and not waste money on a war that was not needed. The Obama administration is already acting on its excellent plan and strategy to convert bank bailouts to equity share, which some critics complain gives too much power to the government. The government is a nonprofit organization that only should look after the health of its country and people, while doing the right thing, which it's doing by buying the toxic assets from banks who started the financial crisis. The republicans should stop playing political games, and if they really said what they believed in, they would have stopped the unnecessary spending on war in Iraq long ago. Although critics claim that by banning lobbyists, democrats and President Obama are missing the crucial distinction between influence peddlers and committed advocates, it's important to remember the scandals that happened during the Republican rule. Even if President Obama has issued an executive order to contain the overbearing and manipulative lobbyists in Washington for now, what he is trying to do is start with a clean slate, review, approve, and maybe even entertain lobbyists who have good intentions and put the needs of the country before the needs of themselves and their backers. Most of the dollar-hungry lobbyists in Washington currently are working only to strengthen their network and will do anything to achieve their goals.

President Obama is a good example of a working-class president who does not take the most powerful job in the world to be a show of prestige. Obama can easily ask the lobbyists to take time off from Washington, as most of his campaign contributions have been from individual contributors spending less than two hundred dollars. All future presidential candidates should follow this campaign funding strategy, so they don't have their hands tied by lobbyists and can't make changes that are beneficial to people. While the government under President Bush and Vice President Dick Cheney included wasting disproportionate amount of money on lobbyists, and acted as lobbyists, helping change laws for their powerful business friends. President Obama wants to change this.

Although the job of a lobbyist started with persuading people associated with public office by acting as an unbiased intermediary to support legislation favorable to the general public, it has become way too complicated and powerful. I totally agree that these lobbyists need to be kicked out of the White House and Washington, so the federal government gets a good grip on the real issues and comes to its own resolutions. Once the Obama administration gets a firm footing in Washington and it feels like it is ready to bring lobbyists back, it should make sure it brings in young and new blood with equally good intentions both for the government and the general public. It's not the lobbyists, but a strong mainstream public sentiment that a government usually heeds.

Some experts claim that the U.S. government is to blame for not setting up high-speed trains. What people need to know is that it's not the government at fault but the underlying airline, automobile, and oil lobbyists who have been keeping the government from setting up the necessary infrastructure. There is no other reason for the government not to sponsor this alternative transportation system in the country; most of Europe and Japan have been enjoying high-speed trains for decades. Had the Supreme Court in 1949 correctly convicted the automotive and oil corporations on monopoly charges, the country would have a high-speed rail system. It is not too late; introducing a high-speed rail system between major cities will decrease gas consumption by automobiles and decrease the price of airline tickets because of competition. Adding an alternate high-speed mode of transportation will not bankrupt the oil, automobile or airline corporations, but the competition will lead to mergers and acquisitions that will benefit these conglomerates. After 9/11, a number of people taking vacations or visiting families during holidays have increasingly hitting the roads even for long-distance trips or not make the trip at all; a high-speed alternative would definitely boost the travel industry.

The American freight train infrastructure is also in dismal condition and the government ought to significantly improve it. The government has to stop heeding the oil and truck lobbyists and do what's right for the environment. Freight trains are way more fuel-efficient than any eighteen-wheelers and expanding the freight railroad network will reduce traffic congestion. Building more highways may decrease traffic congestion but it won't keep the eighteen-wheelers and other freight carrying trucks off the freeways that are causing serious damage to the environment. These disruptive changes maybe bad for the trucking industry, but they will provide a safer and healthier environment for future generations.

What about the three CEOs of the big three auto companies who leased three private jets to fly to Washington to ask for bailout money from the government? Since they had no strategy as to how they would be spending the bailout money, the government might give them, the three stooges were asked to come back with a strategy. With all the media attention the three stooges were getting for the private jet use and lack of a strategy, the next trip to Washington was via their company hybrid cars. They should have made it to Washington on bicycles or Segways to make it more ridiculous and interesting. The only strategy they had was how they got to Washington, how much money they would ask from the government, and how large a bonus they would be getting from the bailout. Although it would be a tragedy to see the three auto giants go bankrupt, it is high time the leaders of the auto industry and other fallen industries take responsibility and rectify the situation.

Instead of giving the bailout money to the auto industry itself and see them waste it, an alternative solution would be to use the bailout money for rebates for citizens who purchased cars from the three companies. This would be a win-win situation for all involved. The U.S. government created a program called Cash for Clunkers to boost the auto sales and get the old low mileage vehicles off the road. This idea isn't doing as well in India, where private airlines are at loggerheads with the government for a bailout. This clearly shows the inefficient nature of a developing government that is not able to handle the issues of an industry in the country during economic downturns.

It is not only the executives that are taking advantage of the system but you probably would not be surprised that a number of greedy labor unions in developed countries that have brought down businesses in the name of better working conditions. While the labor unions were started during the late eighteenth century in the United States in response to a legitimate need to improve working conditions, unions have grown to be extremely powerful and union employees extremely lazy and greedy. According to experts, happy and productive people in a company are nonunion employees and vice-versa. As with lobbyists, it is time for President Obama to get rid of the lethargic and gluttonous labor unions and review the labor laws that have led to the downfall of the Detroit auto industry. Labor unions active in the auto industry should recognize that their dismantling is the only way to save the industry.

Labor unions are nonexistent or not as powerful in developing countries like India because of the uneducated labor force and huge employment market. The governments in those countries should temporarily back the labor unions so industries improve the working conditions of its employees while keeping them competitive.

There are good and bad apples distributed all over the world in both developed and developing countries. Careful government intervention is needed to remove the bad apples and let them face the consequence of a fair and unbiased punishment. Some bad apples do not break the law but become too greedy, pushy, and powerful; the rottenness in this type of bad apple should be carefully removed so it does not spread to the good apples. This usually works well in developed countries but not in developing countries since the apples in the government in developing countries are bad themselves, and they work with other influential bad apples to make sure they are not removed from the tree.

The relationship between the government and the financial system is that of parents and kids. Even if the kids behave badly, the parents get angry but still have to support them. The Federal Reserve learned this once during Great Depression and again when it let wild kid Lehman Brothers go bankrupt. Aside from talented CEOs like Pete Peterson who turned around the company once upon a time and saw record profits, the company was mired in extremely competitive internal environment that led to constant power struggles making it ever so dysfunctional. The parents were so angry that they did not take any action when this bad kid behaved badly; it was a lesson to the others. Governments in developed world have followed this example and provided bailouts to a number of financial companies in their countries, so as to sustain the world economic balance that would otherwise be ruined. The governments in other developed countries also have followed the example of carefully denying the bailout benefits to certain companies, for example the Swedish government didn't bail out automobile giant Saab. The governments are doing the right thing by not blindly giving the bailout package to anyone asking for it and carefully reviewing each case before helping them out.

Although the United States and India have adopted a similar approach to a bailout plan, some European countries are adopting a different technique called *Kurzarbeit* (short work). This is a great approach, and all countries should adopt this scheme by which employees' hours are cut rather than lay them off, and the government pays the difference in wage instead of paying unemployment benefits. It is a great scheme that allows employers to lower costs without increasing the ranks of the unemployed.

While the U.S. government does an exceptional job helping the unemployed by providing benefits that have amounted to $80 billion during these turbulent economic times, its developed counterparts in Europe provide the most generous unemployment benefits to their citizens. Such benefits are alarmingly low or nonexistent in most developing countries. It is time for the United States to update the unemployment insurance program to accommodate an option that would allow an employee who would otherwise be laid off to continue to work but be paid by and receive health insurance from the government. The employee continues to be productive, keeps up with technology, and doesn't suffer the jolt of termination. For the developing countries to provide these amenities will take a huge effort; India faces a huge task of restructuring its benefits program in a comprehensive manner.

The U.S. government also runs a program called Social Security, which is a social welfare and insurance program that includes disability and health insurance for the aged and disabled. The program is funded through taxes on employers, employees, and the self-employed. In 2004, the U.S. government paid $500 billion in social security benefits, making Social Security the largest government program and expense. As the baby boomers enter retirement, the government will have to draw on a trust fund to cover the benefits. Instead of touching the trust fund, the government should change the program's structure to increase the payroll tax to employers and stop paying social security to a family, especially if the spouse is earning a social security check. If the government intends to keep the program going, it should also increase the retirement age by five years. Critics of the social security system claim it distributes wealth from the poor to the rich since workers below social security wage base pay a higher percentage of their wages toward social security. To keep this pyramid scheme going, the government should also set a wage limit for people collecting social security, so the rich who don't need the social security assistance would not be able to participate in the program.

Federal government employees have a separate Federal Employee Retirement System and the Civil Service Retirement System. If federal government employees were treated as any other baby boomers and put into the Social Security system, hundreds of millions of dollars would be saved. Just moving the federal retirement plan called the Thrift Savings Plan to the Social Security system will save over fifty million dollars. Why aren't these easy, cost-effective changes being made? Tampering with Social Security is very political and results in a lot of outrage from baby boomers, but if changes were slowly introduced, they would be accepted.

The Medicare and Medicaid programs that cover medical costs of the elderly and low-income families should be restructured and scaled back, so the government can pay for them with payroll taxes and not have to dig into the current account. These programs should be merged with the public option of health care coverage. Creative ideas that positively affect a significant number of citizens should always be given priority putting bureaucracy and politics in the back burner.

Although the government has been running the Social Security program for a long time, the Indian government had no interest in promoting a social security program until 2006, when it started formulating draft legislation for promoting care, maintenance, and protection of senior citizens. It spent about $5 million for various programs for senior citizens that year, which is a meager amount when you consider that there are 80 million senior citizens living in the country. Age-old custom and tradition in India dictates that the family takes care of its elderly until they die, but as times have changed, so have the customs and tradition. With changing times, the government-proposed legislation to provide need-based maintenance, some level of financial security, pension, setting up a well-equipped ward in each district hospital, and at least one old-age home in each district. As the economy in India has progressed, family culture has changed—no more joint families and no more families staying at the same place. Senior citizens have been left alone by the family and are in need of care. Again the Indian government has to spend substantially more on the social security program to be on par with developed countries; one way for the government to circumvent the bureaucracy and the corrupt system is to directly fund a number of efficient nonprofit organizations that are actively working on a wide variety of senior citizen programs.

Although one could argue that pure socialism or pure communism or pure capitalism is better, but a society with a mixture of each in certain areas would be best. Pure socialism would give rise to less motivated workers, pure communism would lead to a poor state, and pure capitalism would lead to overly greedy entrepreneurs and executives. But a combination of all these would provide a win-win situation for the government and the people. For an almost perfect government, the three mixtures should not be a set percentage but rather a dynamic combination that could be changed based on the need of the country and its people, giving everybody a fair advantage.

Governments with pure forms of these types of economic organization have tumbled during various economic cycles but have consistently recovered or have made huge economic strides when they combined the three styles in varying proportions into their economic policies. Capitalism reigns in most of the developed world, and it flourishes with good regulation enforcement from their governments, which step in as needed during economic downturn cycle creating a mixture of capitalism and socialism. In contrast, most developing countries are predominantly socialist or communist with brief periods of capitalism mixed in to keep up with the developed world. The socialist, communist, or capitalist regimes in these countries can be clearly spotted by the number of government-sponsored enterprises. In a developed country like the United States, government-sponsored enterprises are kept to a minimum.

It is extremely important for the developing and underdeveloped countries to move toward forming a capitalist state that will help them stride into the next phase in their economic chapter. While capitalism is important for economic growth, it is crucial for governments to impose and enforce proper regulations to sustain the growth. One way for the governments of developing countries to ease their step to the next stage of economic growth is by creating strategies in their economic plans to slowly relinquish control of the government-sponsored enterprises. Giving up control of these enterprises gradually only means increased access to capital for these enterprises and that provides more jobs and tax revenues. Increased tax revenues from these private sector enterprises will enable the governments to provide subsidies for the poor and step in to regain control or at least help any enterprises during economic crisis. The primary purpose of government-sponsored enterprises is to create jobs, provide supplies at affordable prices to low-income public, and be the market enabler for innovation. These can be achieved by the private sector if the government provides a balancing act in its regulations to ease the opening of private sectors and at the same time make sure these private companies don't take undue advantage of the system.

In the United States, government-sponsored enterprises have been limited to the housing and farming markets and are intended to improve their efficiency and ease the financial flow in these markets. Government sponsorship of over $15 billion per year for farming over the last decade pushed the average farm household income to match or exceed other household incomes in the country. In India over 150,000 debt-ridden farmers have committed suicide in the same period of time. In quiet contrast, during the Great Depression, the American government helped farmers by buying the farmers' surplus growth and selling it on international markets, implementing regulations for soil conservation to improve farm yields, and introducing several programs to lend a hand to farmers pay their mortgages. The bottom line is that it's not enough for the government to introduce programs for the benefit of its citizens—it must follow up to make sure all the programs are executed to perfection and benefit citizens not the government crooks. While the U.S. federal government paid to build housing projects all over the country in the 1930s as a way to clear out the slums, today these subsidized government projects have given rise to violence, drug use, and prostitution. This clearly shows government-sponsored enterprises or programs don't work, and these enterprises and programs should be transferred to private sector enterprises, especially in developing countries. Programs like the farmer loan waiver in India should be given to nonprofit organizations, changing hands and money directly from the top central government to the nonprofit organizations so as to stop corrupt government officials all along the hierarchy from gobbling the money secured for these essential programs.

The Indian banking sector is in the same situation due to nationalization. Over 90 percent of the banking business is controlled by the government, and banks lack the skilled manpower, growth capital, risk management practices, and even technology to keep up with global standards. The largest commercial banks in India were nationalized because the central government wanted to create an authoritarian financial system based on a socialist regime. The Indian government should move out of its socialist mindset and more into the capitalist mindset if its goal is to achieve significant economic growth in the next five to ten years. This does not mean the government has to relinquish complete control of these banks, but rather it should sell its majority stake to other private sector banks that will help raise capital and bring in talent of global standards to keep up with the next phase of fiscal expansion. The Indian government does not have enough big time visionaries who can put together a growth plan for these banks to compete with foreign banks in the country. Economic liberalization in the country has opened up doors for a number of major foreign banks, but the government has to give up control of at least some of the banks to help growth and allow these domestic banks to be able to compete with the foreign banks on a larger scale.

Experts claim nationalized banks in India have protected the country from the global economic recession of the twentieth century that was caused by the mortgage crisis; critics correctly see this reasoning as bullshit because the mortgage industry in India is insignificant compared to developed countries. The governments of these developing countries can just blindly follow the business strategies of the developed countries and still make significant sustained economic growth that will far exceed its current expectations and actual numbers. The public sector undertaking banks need brand image upgrade because they are perceived as incapable of managing the next economic leap, but the central and state governments need a huge image upgrade and reality check because they have been unable to manage the current economic growth let alone prepare for the next one. The governments in these developing and underdeveloped countries need to take risks that are a little outside their comfort zone, make mistakes but quickly learn from them, and be able to manage chaos successfully—that will help them reach the next level of accomplishment.

Even with so much government help, over 20 percent of all minors in the United States are living under the poverty line, which is the highest in the developed world. The standard of living of the bottom 10 percent in the United States was the second lowest in a developed country. Experts believe that one of the main reasons for poverty in the United States is the de-industrialization that occurs as the country shifts from manufacturing to service-oriented jobs. But one would have to disagree with this since the percentage of the shift is very low; it would seem that one of the main reasons for poverty in the country is due to the fact that about 20 percent of the population is too disabled to work. Even though money is not everything in life, these disabled but amazing people should be able to lead a wonderful life and to make it happen more and more charitable organizations should donate generously to their cause. There are other people living in poverty who are really lazy and responsible for their own actions. One doesn't have to show any pity on them and only should feel bad for them that they are not motivated to better their lives. The other kinds of people in poverty are not lazy but work in minimum wage jobs and give both their jobs and family everything they have. They are in a transition phase to be somewhere better in life either through education or experience and are ambitious.

In a developing country like India, the poverty rate and conditions of people living in poverty are more dismal than in any developed country. Without government help, the poor and needy are left to fend for themselves, and life becomes a tale of survival of the fittest. These people lead tragic lives, working hard for about $2 a day to provide three meals daily to themselves and their families. As in any country, there are tales of people who have seen their lives change from living in poverty to leading a rich life either by a stroke of luck or through hard work.

In the United States, homelessness could be attributed to factors like mental illness, physical disability, and foster kids who leave foster homes when they turn eighteen. In India, it has been due to government corruption, not enough government assistance, and extremely low wages. Homelessness in developed countries is at a minimum not only due to the people's efforts to strive hard to be successful and higher minimum wages but also because of government assistance. There is so much corruption in the Indian government that these greedy and low-life politicians don't even spare the homeless programs. They wouldn't think twice to fake their eligibility to grab land meant for affordable housing. After the economic liberalization of the 1990s, the country has seen so much wealth that has turned a number of materialistic people to go to extreme lengths to snatch anything they can from anybody. If the people in the government cannot control this corrupt attitude, the country is going to be in great trouble if and when the next wave of economic success hits the country.

Similar to homelessness, the statistics for domestic violence in the developed world versus the developing world are drastically different. One in four women in developed countries suffer physical or sexual abuse, whereas two out of three married women in developing countries endure physical or sexual abuse from their husbands. Law in this country doesn't mean jack since these abusive men, their family, and society in general can easily overpower these laws and it's up to the abused victims and women's activist groups to stand up to them. Women in this country need to understand that they have as equal an opportunity as any men to lead a respectable life that does not involve any kind of abuse from their partners or family members. They should stand up for their rights by denouncing the abuse from their partners and by going to authorities. Most women in India and many other developing and underdeveloped countries silently suffer abuse from their partners either due to a social stigma that a man and a woman are married for life regardless of how their partners treat them or due to the economic factor that they don't earn any income because they are stay at home wives or moms and are afraid to be independent while at the same time be successful. While these abusive men are taking advantage of their social and economic status in the society, it is up to these women and their family members to say enough is enough and put an end to it both by reporting to authorities and moving on from abusive relationships in their lives.

One can see that most of the social issues in the developed world and the developing world are similar, but the developing world is decades behind and usually takes a little longer to resolve their economic issues because of a number of intertwined factors that are harder to resolve for a developing mindset. Even though the three different mindsets of the developed world, the developing world, and the underdeveloped world were similar in their mindsets and social and economic conditions centuries ago, the developed world at some point broke away and took off in this never ending marathon. Now it's up to the developing and the underdeveloped worlds to resolve as many of their socioeconomic issues as quickly as possible and in the best possible way, so they can catch up with the developed world—maybe even overtake it someday. It sometimes seems like the developing countries especially the emerging markets have the ability to make it to the circle of the developed world, but the governments for some reason don't want the added responsibility that comes with being in that special circle. It is pathetic to see their half-ass efforts to be called a developed country so that they can boast of their achievement but failing to accept the responsibility that comes with it.

Chapter 3
My Wallet Is Empty, Is Yours?

Along with the government, a stable, responsible, and powerful financial system is required for the better functioning of a country; it clearly differentiates the making of the developed and the developing worlds. The U.S. financial system recently has been going through crisis due to the sub-prime mortgage issues and the tumbling of the banking system. But since a government's wallet is never empty, it can jump in to manage the economic crisis. Various governments all around the world are experiencing this situation to varying degrees, and although you can't just snap out of an economic crisis, the least you could do is shake it off and move on.

The GDP per capita of the United States is significantly higher than its developing counterparts, but there have been concerns regarding its national/international debt, mortgage crisis, banking crisis, and Social Security liabilities. All these issues are having ripple effects all over the world, including in India, where the real estate market has tumbled, along with its software services market because of cuts in foreign investment. While the U.S. public debt is the world's largest, relative to the nation's GDP, it's roughly equivalent to other developed nations in Europe. Why are critics making a big hoopla about the size of the U.S. public debt but not about the economic recovery or the universal health care? While measures need to be taken to bring down the public debt, it is not going to happen overnight and definitely not during tough economic times. On the other hand, it has been argued and shown during the Great Depression that intentionally leaving the budget unbalanced to a certain degree boosts demand and results in economic recovery. The complex economic jigsaw puzzle falls into place when the government takes the most effective actions at the right time to repay as much public debt as possible without disrupting other economic factors.

While both Bush and Cheney have retired to their ranches after creating a whole lot of mess during their stay in the White House, the Obama administration has an overwhelming task of stabilizing the economy, as well as managing the huge budget deficit. It is a little hard to comprehend that states would cut their budgets, including education, and lay off government employees, while the federal government is striving to create thousands of jobs by funding a number of infrastructure development projects. So the practical thing to do would be to cancel unimportant infrastructure development programs and fund state-sponsored education and other core programs cut due to budget shortfall. The federal government should create a structure and efficiency team to analyze all the programs run by the federal and state governments, and fund only those programs that are important for either federal or state governments. Most of the state government budget woes have been due to the economic crisis, which meant less tax revenue.

There were times when the U.S. debt was less than $100 million, and President Andrew Jackson even paid the debt off one year. While President Obama will not be able to pay the entire debt off, he has a plan to significantly reduce it. President Jackson paid off the debt during regular economic times by vetoing a number of federal development projects, which is not a good thing to do especially during tough economic times. If a government keeps paying off its debt, then the country's development stalls significantly which will undermine its growth and put its economy on a much slower path. Obama's strategic plan is to create a perfect balance of all three: pay off as much debt as possible, put economy on an upward trend, and not increase taxes for middle-income America. So everybody's asking the question how the federal government is going to pay any debt off without a tax increase? The catch is the government did not say it wouldn't increase taxes applicable to high-net-worth individuals. This makes perfect sense because 5 percent of the population is very high-net-worth individuals who control 95 percent of the nation's total personal wealth, so increasing taxes to this segment of the population would yield an astronomical amount of tax revenue. This is exactly the kind of change that America needs and that President Obama assured voters he would bring during his campaign. It's the kind of change that Republicans dreaded as these successful strategies would put them way behind in the political race. The Republicans also turned a blind eye to the major corporations that take advantage of offshore tax havens and cost the government close to $100 billion a year. President Obama wants the business-politics relationship to be more like a two-way relationship in which the government helps businesses during tough economic times, and the businesses should either move away from tax havens or face higher taxes. This is how it should be, and it's a brazen hypocrisy that businesses and the Republicans are opposing these much-needed measures.

The United States didn't become a developed economy overnight or without careful planning. It started by transforming the agriculture sector from a major GDP contributor to a high-yielding sector. The transformation is amazing, and India has a lot to learn from the U.S. agriculture sector in terms of how the government helped the farmers get to where they are now and how the sector transformed itself into one of the best-yielding sectors in the country and in the world. The learning can happen only if the Indian government and the people in the agriculture sector are willing to make the changes that are necessary. The path to this change is going to be hard and long since the government and the people of the developing country of India have to be educated and trained consistently to make this sacrifice. Motivation and the desire to make this sacrifice have to come from within and cannot be taught, hence all one can do is provide the path and hope for the change with fingers crossed.

After gaining independence, India was filled with political corruption and at an economic standstill until the economic liberalization in the early 1990s by the then Prime Minister Narasimha Rao and Finance Minister Manmohan Singh. They established the computer-based trading system and opened the equity markets to foreign institutional investors in India, resulting in an investment increase of billions of dollars. These two extensively educated ministers had a shared vision of changing the landscape of Indian economy significantly amidst criticism and opposition from the simplex-minded politicians and people who were scared of the change it would bring to the country. Even though most changes to the economy would be positive, they were scared of the negative effects of this change. These simplex-minded politicians and people wanted the traditional approach to changing the economy that would take centuries to transform India into a regional economic power. Although Singh has been portrayed as a weak political leader, it is educated progressive leaders like him who have the ability to change the developing mindset to a developed one. It was an impressive change that was only expected from him with no prior political experience and hence no political baggage. It is only these kinds of leaders that can change the political and economic scene and lead India to the road of recovery that had been battered for centuries during the British rule.

Another progressive and Harvard-educated leader who has been working on changing the social-economic scenario in India is the current Finance Minister P. Chidambaram. But like any politician working in a coalition government in a developing country, the well-intentioned Chidambaram is mired in controversies that include a $15 billion farmer-loan waiver scheme, which has led to public interest litigation. Damned if you do and damned if you don't is what it feels like when your political foes are hell-bent on bringing you down and it is in one's best interest to keep on doing the right thing. Rather than just introducing a farmer-loan waiver scheme, Chidambaram should concentrate on restructuring the entire agriculture sector to help transform it to a high-yielding business.

The U.S. public has lost complete trust in the financial sector because of the outrageous executive pay and scandals that have further ruined the economy. Free-market capitalism is not about screwing your clients, and it was right to let Lehman Brothers go bankrupt after they were hit badly by sub-prime mortgage debt. Public feelings changed from bitterness to anger when they heard that the greedy and shameless executives were taking hundreds of millions of dollars in undeserved pay package even after they knew that their company was going down. It is time for Wall Street to change from the dog-eat-dog mindset that goes from backstabbing partners to getting the most bang from its clients' buck and work toward creating long-term sustainability even if it means lower profits. Although these financial companies may have taken advantage of the government regulation loopholes, the way the greedy executives are acting feels like one is looking at a developing or an underdeveloped country. The immense amounts of selfishness and greed these people are displaying in front of the world have put many fellow citizens and the country to shame. Until the financial system recovers and successfully stands on its feet, the government needs to step in and create a mixture of socialist and capitalist form of banking system by nationalizing banks and giving them control of the monetary supply system.

As if the country's financial system collapse was not enough to put on a black face, Bernie Madoff, the former chairman of the NASDAQ stock exchange, was arrested for committing the largest investor fraud ever by a single individual, with liabilities of over $50 billion, wiping out entire life savings of a number of rich all around the world. This crook was running a ponzi scheme for over two decades and made a number of billionaire investors and charities believe that he was investing intelligently with a significant rate of return. This high society criminal thought that he would run the notorious scheme until his death, but his sons turned him in after realizing they didn't want to be responsible for something that they were not aware of until the day before. This behavior is so far beyond greed that words can't describe it—utter madness is not even close. It is surprising and rewarding to see two individuals who have the same DNA as their gluttonous father, have the conscience to turn the parent in as soon as they get the information about the scheme. Whether they realized it or not, they also helped a number of other potential investors who would have invested in Madoff not make the same mistake as others already affected.

That's what I thought when I read about the fraud but after investigating more about the Madoff family, it is hard to believe that wife Ruth and the kids were out of loop of Bernie's investment scheme. It is especially hard to understand Ruth's lack of knowledge because she usually kept close tabs everyday on Bernie and the kids. She was there 24/7 with him, at the office, home, countless business meetings, and vacations. There's no way she could have not known. It was a way for Bernie to go down by himself and save the family from jail time. There is nothing Bernie can do to save the family from embarrassment and humiliation, which they truly deserve. A lot of money just disappeared and the family should be held accountable since they were all working in Bernie's company. Moral here is, never trust anybody regardless of what their position is in society and fearlessly go after them if you sense them doing something unethical, especially when people's life savings are involved.

President Obama needs to clean up the SEC, which was aware of Madoff's Ponzi scheme way before the media brought it to light but did nothing to stop him. There's too much hand shaking between Wall Street and the SEC, and cleaning up the SEC is the only way to clean up Wall Street. Even better would be for a secondary government organization like the FBI or the CIA to keep a constant close eye on SEC, so they know they have to be clean all the time. Okay, time to move on from the Madoff madness.

As the economy is in a recession, it is also time for the professional sports players and team owners in the country to take a look at their hefty pay packages. This includes three major sports areas of football, baseball, and basketball, and minor sports areas of car racing, soccer, hockey, and golf. The relevant sports authorities and sponsors should take responsibility during these difficult times and make adjustments to player salaries and prize money. These responsible actions during difficult times will help them later as the economy gets better when fans return the favor by spending more money on games and merchandise.

Free-market capitalism also means powerful conglomerates enjoying more than 50 percent worldwide market segment share should be careful about their business ethics so as to not get sued by its lesser-known competitors for monopolistic business practices. While the United States long ago implemented and strictly enforces laws against monopolistic business practices, the governing agencies in the developed world in Europe are slowly enforcing the already existing tough anti-monopolistic business practices. These contrasts sharply with antimonopoly laws in a developing country like India, where antimonopoly laws not only don't exist, the monopolistic businesses enjoy the luxury of holding hands with the government to ensure any laws that come into affect will not hamper them. This government-monopolistic business handholding happened in Europe for centuries as it's happening now in developing countries but with a dirty catch. While the European governments had granted monopolies on all kinds of manufacturing and trade to their trustworthy citizens in return for cash, interest, or a share of the profits, the politicians in developing countries are using these fiscal revenues for personal gain. The European governments let the monopolistic industries remain in private hands without nationalizing them but used the steady stream of revenue, which was sometimes as high as one-third of the overall government budget, to significantly improve the country's infrastructure. The politicians in developing countries are squandering this dirty money on personal amusement and luxury instead of spending it on worthy causes for their country. A number of family-owned Indian business conglomerates like Reliance, Tata, and Birla have monopolistic holds in a number of sectors, but the weak government and judicial system are in no position to hold them accountable for their improper business practices. There has to be an international governing body to whip a government that is involved in fixing business models for unfair kickbacks.

While the Indian government has instilled some laws to curb business monopolies, it has still a long way to go since it has not put any concrete laws to curb mergers and acquisitions (M&A) that would lead to monopolies. A huge part in restraining big businesses from taking over a sector of the industry to enjoy ridiculous pricing models and exorbitant profits is to enforce anti-M&A laws like the U.S. government did in the early twentieth century in response to Rockefeller's hold on the oil industry and Morgan's hold on the banking industry. India has to put forth antimonopoly and anti-M&A laws and vigorously enforce them to ensure economic efficiency and growth since fair competition from a number of businesses in a sector leads to innovation and economic growth. With the government's help, the Ambanis, Tatas, and Birlas are enjoying the ride, while the country's growth stagnates.

In addition to laying out effective measures for eradicating the monopolistic price fixing problem, the Indian government also needs to pull out a successful formula to increase the efficiency of the agriculture sector. It doesn't matter if India ranks second in the world in terms of agricultural output because it is sucking up the labor force and poor irrigation facilities and heavy dependence on rainfall, lack of use of technology and modern agricultural practices, inefficient finance and marketing services are all making it a low-yielding sector. To turn things around, it is not enough to change agricultural procedures because most of the labor force in this sector would lose their jobs and would need to be trained, educated, and offered jobs in other sectors or else the unemployment rate would multiply, which would stall the economic development.

Economic liberalization may have put a number of Indian companies on the global map, but cheaper imports from China and other countries have threatened the industry. Companies have repositioned themselves by squeezing costs, relying on innovation, and implementing a new low cost technology. Companies in developing economies should have a very fair balance between quality and profitability especially when exporting to developed economies, as poor quality and reliability won't work in the long run. Take for example, Tata Motors, India's leading automobile company, which just released the low-cost Tata Nano brand of cars, selling for a minimum of $2,500. This would only fit the developing markets but would not come close to passing the safety and emissions standards of the developed markets. While it is important for Tata Motors to bring the cheapest car to the developing and underdeveloped markets, they also have to realize they can't neglect safety and reliability standards, even if those governments don't have them.

It is happening in the high-tech sector in a number of emerging and developing economies where schools, colleges, and parents are cranking out graduates in record numbers faster than they are ready. Some of the major Indian IT corporations are dueling with multinational conglomerates for a piece of the global IT pie but they are not able to deliver to the expectations because it is taking a lot longer for these graduates to get used to higher quality and reliability standards. With economic liberalization and continued investments by multinational companies, these Indian IT companies have thrived, but it also has created an economic divide that has resulted in the rich getting enormously richer and the middle-class striving to survive in an inflated market. Even though the number in middle-class has grown significantly, the poor still struggle extremely but a number of the rich have enjoyed tremendous success and have made it to the world's top ten billionaires list. For the economic imbalance to end and for India to be on top of the world economic map, the poor have to get more motivated to thrive with help from the government that creates a much more favorable environment for the poor. Due to the booming Indian economy and lack of capability to sustain growth, the government made a wise decision to change the Foreign Direct Investment (FDI) policy to allow 100 percent of FDI in various development ventures, including housing/commercial building, hotels/resorts, city infrastructures, hospitals, and educational institutions. With the economy in recession in the United States, the software services sector in India has been affected by extended budget cuts by U.S. companies that rely on software services companies in India. The ripple effect has been seen in the slowing real estate market as demand for housing has reduced with wary consumers tightening their budgets. The effect on India would not be as great as seen in the United States since it still has a growing pool of talented, educated, and cheap labor that the U.S. corporations want to take advantage of for positive economic benefits.

Although the current economic downturn in the United States may not seem as bad as the Great Depression of the 1930s, the government has the ability to see the big picture and hence has introduced the gigantic economic bailout package to avoid another depression or what would be called the great recession. With the dollar amount in today's financial crisis much bigger than during the Great Depression, a total financial collapse and the realization of recession would be much more devastating with enormous consequences not only in the United States but in the entire world. In terms of unemployment, it may not be as bad as during the Great Depression because the computer evolution created more jobs than during earlier times. Although the situation in 2009 is similar to that of the Great Depression in terms of the banking system collapse and stock market crash, aid from the government seems to be reaching further than before and that would be the reason for the current situation would not go beyond a recession. The government has to do everything possible to maintain a balanced and stable economy, avoid a total collapse of the system, and boost to consumer confidence. Along with the government, high net worth individuals, despite their dwindling portfolios, need to invest in businesses so they can create more jobs that will help the economy bounce back.

The Wall Street crash of 1929 was the most devastating in the history of the United States, and the depression led to a lot of financial reforms and new trading regulations. One can expect a number of reforms and regulations at the end of this recession. The beauty of the economic cycle is that it lets all the unstable markets fall during recession and at the end of the recession, with help from the renewed regulations, the entire system stands up stronger and healthier. It is the responsibility of the government to make significant change in regulations that will decide how fast and how strong the economy is going to be once the recession is over. It is up to President Barack Obama and his competitive team to bring the country out of shambles.

Although experts claim that the securities acts of 1933 and 1934 were the reaction to Ivar Kreuger, European entrepreneur and financial genius dubbed the greatest swindler in all history, but Kreuger only helped hasten Congressional action to protect future American investors. This financial genius not only had impressive business models for his companies but also advised on new financial models to governments and leaders all over the world. The tragedy was that he took undue advantage of his genius mind to swindle money from American investors even during the market crash and caused at least two major banks to go bankrupt. Kreuger and Madoff point out that just because someone is either a financial genius or has held one of the highest offices in Wall Street, investors shouldn't automatically trust them with their money. Instead, investors should demand every detail of their investments and keep tabs on them. It is absurd that many people believe investors, auditors and bankers should also be blamed for the Kreuger and Madoff scandals. These swindlers are solely responsible for fiddling with the investors' money while the investors, auditors, bankers, and regulatory authorities should have been proactive in demanding detailed information from these high-profile cheaters. These swindlers are solely responsible because they successfully played into the psyche of the naïve investors by offering them substantial dividends and held the auditors and bankers at bay by advertising their high-profile status while hiding their ulterior motives. While the high profile swindlers lavished on investors' money, they also made themselves inaccessible to unaware investors, blindsided auditors and bankers by locking themselves in remote locations and giving as little information as possible about the investments but kept them happy on a short-term basis by paying constant dividends.

Do you think allowing the investment and commercial banks to be consolidated led to the 2007 sub-prime mortgage financial crisis? That's what critics who want to blame the government for the trough in economic cycle want us to believe. Although almost every business takes calculated risks to grow and expand their revenue, this sub-prime mortgage risk taken by many financial firms has been a costly one for both the businesses and their clients who have lost their homes to the mortgage mess. The CEOs and executives of these companies took advantage of the booming economy, the real estate market, and the regulation loophole for their own personal gains; when the market and their firms tanked, they were only concerned about themselves and not about their clients or their firms. Economists and financial experts say the sub-prime mortgage crisis and the recession during the first decade of the twentieth century to anywhere from former Presidents Reagan and Bush to former Federal Reserve chief Alan Greenspan pointing out specific microeconomic deregulation laws that led to the financial dip. But they fail to point out the lack of policing efforts by the SEC and the companies that exploited them. These economists and financial experts seemingly fail to see the macroeconomic picture at the level of an economic cycle where usually a government deregulation or increase in demand leads to a bubble, and when the system is unable to sustain the bubble, it bursts. There are always businesses that find loopholes in financial laws to increase their bottom line, and it's important for the government to flex certain laws by deregulation while tightening the laws in other areas to make sure these businesses don't exploit the system. Instead of pointing fingers, the economists and financial experts should come up with constructive analysis that will help the government build a bullet-proof system but let the gradual growth of the economy happen. A free-market system without government regulations will only result in economic chaos with everybody trying to screw each other in the name of free-market capitalism.

After the public confidence in the securities market eroded in the wake of a series of corporate scandals that brought down the likes of Enron, World-Com, Tyco, and Adelphia, the federal government reacted appropriately by bringing new Sarbanes-Oxley legislation into affect in 2002. This legislation helps keep close tabs on public company boardrooms, management, and also the accounting firms that audit the companies. A number of businesses that usually conform to standard corporate governance practices are very dissatisfied by the new legislation since compliance is expensive. The good guys of business practices should stop complaining about the new legislation adding more paperwork since these new regulations are required to keep the bad guys of business practices in check.

The Sarbanes-Oxley Act should be extended to all private companies, universities, government entities, and nonprofit companies immediately, so the risks of these companies not abiding to corporate governance is reduced and in turn public confidence in nonprofit organizations would increase as a result of these changes. These extensions would increase the likelihood that an employee would be unafraid of being fired if he or she blew the whistle on misappropriations in the organization. Whistleblower protection should be the most important policy implemented in all government entities because public service should be as clean as an obsessed clean freak's color-coordinated wardrobe. Whistleblower protection is doubly important in developing and underdeveloped countries, as poor law enforcement would offer little security against the death threats from the powerful bad guys. It gets worse when the law enforcement is on the side of the bad guys, which is most often the case in developing and underdeveloped countries. Companies in developing and underdeveloped countries along with the governments should draft clear and detailed whistleblower policies to ensure that confidentiality of the whistle blower is maintained by all parties at all times during the time of the investigation. A lot of software services companies in India with major clients in the developed world are still not up to par on corporate governance. While a number of executives of fallen corporations in the United States are spending a significant amount of time in jail for their involvement in accounting scandals, the proceedings of Indian corporate scandals have been dragging on for decades with no resolution in sight. Ratings of Indian corporate governance is half that of the United States. It is high time the Indian government steps in to escalate the issue, so justice can be served as soon as possible.

Cutting taxes to help consumers and heavy government spending to help unemployed revived economic growth after the Great Depression, but this won't be the case after the great recession because the federal government is going to be in cautionary mode to keep the public debt in check. Some experts believe that the tightening of the money supply by the Federal Reserve when markets needed it caused the Great Depression, but this is not absolutely true, as drastically increasing the money supply by the Federal Reserve would have caused inflation and a deeper depression. The real cause of Great Depression was the collapse of banking systems and the stock market. Although one could argue that the government only created jobs by increasing its investments in infrastructure projects, one has to agree that the then government did everything it could within its capability. It is important for middle-class America to understand how much better they have it here compared to their European counterparts because of the hard work of its government.

The government cannot restructure or privatize Social Security because baby boomers are scared to risk their retirement money in a new system run by a free-market capitalist. A mixture of capitalism and socialism is necessary in the United States because people are becoming too skeptical of pure capitalism, and a small percentage of socialism will bring back confidence in the government. Governments in the developed world may have been doing a marvelous job in helping their countries recover from the dip of the financial cycles, but not anymore unless they cut back on other ever-growing payment services. Would you rather see your government go bankrupt or see them raise taxes or cut payouts? Would you rather see your government increase its dependence on foreign sources to fund the current account that will give the foreign sources an unfair advantage to cut deals with the government or otherwise? Can you imagine what would happen if these foreign sources that fund the public debt had voting rights to influence the country's internal policies? These are the questions that a government needs to ask its people to help grow and maintain the economy, and although most developing countries may use similar policy strategies, it may not work as well because of loose enforcement and extensive corruption. As stated earlier, the Indian government needs to tighten its enforcement techniques and put its anticorruption team in full force, so it can be a fair, powerful, and balanced government to its people.

Although it is a simple economic equation for government to maintain low inflation, high economic growth, and low unemployment by using monetary and fiscal policies, a number of social and political factors make it extremely complex. The developed world does a better job than the developing world of successfully maneuvering through this complex social and political maze because they not only understand the economic algorithms but also have mastered the social and political psyche. If the Indian government does not have the best strategies, it needs to work with the think tanks to come up with the best policies that will work for the benefit of the country. The think tanks should reduce redundancy by collaborating with each other on common research goals. India's multiparty system doesn't enable the best visionary leader to come to power. With the educated middle-class expanding, they must do their best to bring an educated and visionary leader to power in every single election, so India does not have to stall and suffer both politically and economically.

The U.S. Department of Treasury manages the government revenue and collects federal taxes by maintaining a Federal Reserve Bank account. The Treasury also prints and mints all paper currency, stamps, bonds, and coins that the Federal Reserve distributes to financial institutions. It is like having a money tree in the government's backyard, but the government has to balance everything in terms of economic equations and also with commonsense. Just because they have a money tree in the backyard, they don't pluck it every time they need the money. Instead they go to their family members and neighbors who lend to them. Computers run through complex mathematical equations to come up with the amount to be borrowed and the best effective formulas usually result in numbers beneficial to everyone.

The Indian government started the Planning Commission to formulate the country's socioeconomic five-year plans, but unless the government incorporates major plans to improve the infrastructure and address environmental concerns, the mere existence of the commission should be questioned. Do you really need a commission that is usually headed by a corrupt and inept leader to identify how net tax proceeds should be distributed between the central and state governments? What a complete waste of taxpayers' money! Instead the government should hire a private independent organization to do the research and provide the report directly to the finance minister.

In most developing countries, infrastructure development should never be handled by the public sector as it is beleaguered by corruption and bureaucratic inefficiencies. India's budget investment on infrastructure development in power, construction, transportation, telecommunications, and real estate has been way less than 10 percent of the GDP; compare that to China's investment of 20 plus percent of its GDP. A successful business conglomerate with enough cash in hand maintains a steady output during economic downturn, so that it is ready when the economy picks up steam. The same applies to infrastructure development in emerging economies. Lack of proper infrastructure has been one of the causes for slower growth rate in emerging economies than what it could be, and therefore the government has to open up infrastructure development to the private sector with help from foreign investors. The Indian government has to step up its infrastructure investments, so that the country can keep up with China or else lose a lot of foreign investments to its neighbor where the government has hired world-renowned foreign infrastructure development teams to rebuild entire infrastructure system in various cities.

Whether it got its name from Walloons, the French-speaking Belgians who settled in the area or the wall that was created to defend against attacks from Native American tribes, Wall Street has become one of the most powerful financial districts in the world. It is unimaginable that once upon a time it was here that traders and speculators gathered under a tree to trade that later became a trading floor where membership costs over three million dollars. While experts are compelled to believe that the brilliant idea of the twenty-four traders to start the New York Stock Exchange (NYSE) was due to the acts of a single man named William Duer, it was actually because of the Panic of 1792, which forced the traders to bring normalcy to the trading system. Duer was taking advantage of the unlimited credit the banking system was extending, but there were a number of other players involved in the triggering of the panic. The traders were quick and bold enough to start the NYSE to make the trading system a little more methodical, but it would take the federal government more than a century to bring regulations to the stock market through the introduction of Securities and Exchange Commission (SEC).

It is hard not to get sucked into the greedy world of free-market capitalism when a commodities exchange like the New York Mercantile Exchange (NYMEX) is located right in the heart of Wall Street, where billions of dollars worth of energy products, metals, and other commodities are traded everyday. How could it not turn your pride and ego to arrogance when prices for some of the commodities all over the world are set by the trading value of these commodities on the NYMEX? Greed for money is not just limited to the developed world but is more so in the developing and the underdeveloped world, where people sometimes will go to extreme lengths to grab a piece of the pie. Economic liberalization in the 1990s got the attention of a stockbroker nicknamed Big Bull in Bombay Stock Exchange (BSE) who persuaded a number of major commercial banks to entrust him with large amounts of funds and who influenced the general course of direction of the BSE Sensex. He swindled banks to the tune of one billion dollars but unlike in a developed country, he was let out on bail after five years and started another scam. It is appalling that none of the bankers or corporate executives involved in both Big Bull scams ever saw the comforts of a jail cell; instead, they are merrily spending their time as though they were never involved in any criminal activity. With India's law enforcement and judicial system showing leniency to these corporate criminals, another scam master nicknamed Bombay Bull siphoned off about half a billion dollars from banks. All suspects are enjoying their time while out on bail. This is a good example of the rotten state the country's financial and regulatory systems are in and it is similar to the situation in a number of other developing and underdeveloped countries. The judicial system in developing countries should take a tougher stance on these corporate thugs; they should not receive preferential treatment or bail, and convictions should be harsh resulting in a considerably longer jail time. People who take advantage of the loopholes in the system for short-term gain clearly know the risks of getting caught, so all these corporate crimes should be considered premeditated.

Low interest rates may have initiated the housing bubble, but it was the uncalculated risks taken by the sub-prime mortgage lenders that led to the collapse. They recklessly gave mortgages to anyone regardless of income level or employment status or credit history. They intended to create huge profits while deliberately causing damage to their clients. When the housing downturn hit different parts of the country, these lenders ran around like fugitives avoiding the wrath of angry victims while telling them to read the fine print in their agreements. When critics blame the gloomy credit crisis on sub-prime mortgage lenders, it is astonishing to see that these lenders don't want to take the blame at all; they say the borrowers didn't have a gun to their head to sign the mortgage papers. Just because they didn't use coercion doesn't make them blameless because they approved mortgages of equal amounts to every single person who walked through the door regardless of whether the person's annual salary was fifteen thousand or a million. Although borrowers should have read all the costly fine print that comes with every outrageous sweet deal, the lenders took unfair advantage of the oblivious customers and approved them for mortgage loans for which they were unqualified.

Homeowners have been unwilling to reduce their selling price after the housing boom resulting in homes-for-sale glut. This puts more homeowners at risk of default and foreclosure. The holders of sub-prime mortgages didn't expect home values to plunge, and when refinancing became difficult, borrowers began defaulting on loans. The credit rating agencies, mortgage brokers, financial institutions, and government regulators also played a major role in the sub-prime mortgage crisis. Instead of risking foreclosure, homeowners should try to sell their homes without any intentions of making profits but at the same time don't have to pay out of their own pockets after the sale.

The Federal Reserve introduced three new tools to address problems created by the sub-prime mortgage crisis to benefit both the financial industry and the affected homeowners. While the free market system may look perfect at its best, crises like the sub-prime mortgage blunder and conglomerate bankruptcies would make even libertarians like Milton Friedman think twice. A mixed economy with government regulation to ensure companies don't take undue advantage of the system is better than a completely free market system that will only result in a street full of corporate thugs and the economic destruction of everyone involved. A mixed economy allows the government to step in during any economic crisis to stabilize the economy even during the trough of a normal business cycle.

What are the two major socioeconomic issues that emerging markets should have to deal with that will help them hop toward the next step of economic freedom? For a country like India, poverty and corruption, compounded by problems of population control, are its two major problems. When you hear that the percentage of people living under the national poverty line reduced from 50 percent to 30 percent in thirty years, you may be ready to give kudos to the government for an excellent job. But before you do, let's investigate a little further shall we? India's population during those thirty years almost doubled to a little over one billion, so the amount of people under the poverty line actually increased by over thirty million. The World Bank should stop praising India for its efforts in poverty reduction because the government efforts are all talk and no action. The bank's aid toward poverty reduction projects should never be delivered to the government but to effective nonprofit charities instead. Since independence, the government has implemented various schemes like the food-for-work program, supplying food at controlled prices, and the national-rural-employment program to alleviate the conditions of the poor without greatly improving quality of life for the poor. When the population living in poverty is in hundreds of millions, programs like food-for-work only helps them to work and eat, but it doesn't bring them out of poverty.

People living in poverty in rural areas that are willing to work and have little or no education are encouraged to move to cities because commercial and industrial businesses need cheap labor. These people cannot afford housing in cities, and this has given rise to slums in all major cities, where poor people create unauthorized shelters using tents, cardboards, or mud huts. Although some people with money continue living in slums to avoid rent and taxes, these places have poor sanitary conditions and poor infrastructure. There are about fifteen million slum dwellers in India. There are no proper bathrooms in these slums, which is a huge public health hazard. With substantial government help and steady growth in economy, poverty and slums will be reduced significantly in the coming twenty-five or so years.

That's what the government claims, but we will have to wait and see if the government will keep up this promise. Alleviating poverty is a long-term goal, and providing education and jobs to the poor will definitely head India toward the path to be a developed country in the near future. To achieve this, it's important to keep the surroundings clean by imposing a hefty fine and jail time on anyone violating the rules. Nonviolent criminals spending time in jail should be put to service cleaning up the mess. These inmates will be able to do a better job of cleaning than the professionals since the government spent over two hundred million dollars on cleaning river Ganges but still failed to decrease the pollution level. This pretend cleaning of the rivers due to corruption has only led to the deaths of thousands of kids living on the banks of the river everyday.

The World Bank should completely circumvent corrupt governments in their poverty reduction projects. Corruption is the main reason why these poverty reduction projects are not working in India, and an anticorruption vaccine needs to be quickly developed to curb this disease that is spreading like a plague in developing and underdeveloped countries. Politicians and public officials often compromise their integrity and their country's security and integrity in order to receive bribes. The main reason for the brave but unreasonable acts of corruption in India and other developing countries is that very little is done to stop it. If there were vigilant watchdogs and dire consequences, this terrible infection could be curbed once and for all. There have been a number of undercover sting operations to expose the corrupt politicians and officials, but people who try to expose these corrupt officials often receive death threats or even get killed. The media and the anticorruption officials should increase their undercover sting operations because this is the most effective way to expose the corrupt officials; consequences for corruption should be strictly enforced.

In a developed country like the United States, talk show hosts debate the political and social issues that plague their country. As in the developed world and parts of the developing world, the media should be independent of the government and should be allowed to make their arguments with strong opinions but based on facts. An independent media can bring the whole story to the public and keep the government as honest as possible. Walter Cronkite, a long-time news anchorman who always had a tell-it-like-it-is policy, had the respect of very many U.S. presidents because of his passionate, strong, and independent personality both in front and off camera. During the course of the Vietnam War, Cronkite visited the battlefield and reported to the public audience that the United States was at a stalemate. President Lyndon Johnson responded that he had lost the support of Middle America since he had lost Cronkite's support. Always state your facts, blurt your opinions whether for or against your government, tell it like it is, and always make it count.

The independence of the U.S. news media was clearly displayed during the Nixon administration when the country's largest print and television outlets extensively covered the Watergate scandal, which involved the president. The news media should not constantly blurt out their extreme ideologies just to increase ratings. Sometimes the U.S. news and sports media take it a little too far with their personal political negative comments and analyzing sportspersons' personal lives, which should be done with a balanced approach. In a developing country, reporting against the government, especially the president, will result in death threats against the reporter or editor or even career suicide; in a dictatorship it's a death sentence for the reporter. Indian journalists and talk show hosts should follow the American example and debate the significant and insignificant social issues that afflict the Indian subcontinent, so that the citizens are aware of these issues. The governments that control the media are only afraid of their people, and this is a good indication to the people that they can overcome and overthrow the fearful undemocratic governments by being strong.

It is not only up to the Indian media and the anticorruption unit to make a difference but also to people to resist giving bribes to corrupt officers or catch them in the act. Although resisting them would lead to other unwanted actions by these officials, catching them in the act and handing over the proof to the media would be a good way to put them on the spot. Corruption has driven poor farmers to commit suicide because the banks want kickbacks when the farmers are already struggling with enormous debt. Some state and local government officials have been crowned as the worst offenders both in terms of lawlessness and corruption for stealing millions of dollars worth of flood relief money that should have been distributed to the poor and needy. There is definitely something wrong with the core system in India because a statewide scandal that stole over $280 million worth from agriculture over a period of twenty years went undetected. An uneducated scoundrel of a minister of one of the poorest and least educated states in the country was scamming his people for over two decades, and when it came to light, instead of sending him to jail, he was made the railway minister in the central government. If India wants its core system to change for the better, it needs to stop these actions of installing corrupt ministers in the government, which not only curbs progress but also is detrimental to its stability. How can a country be secure and its people able to trust the government when even its arms negotiations end up with government officials receiving millions of dollars in kickbacks? Failure in the system makes the people not trust in their elected representatives and this disconnection will ultimately lead to an ineffective government that will continuously stall progress.

India has to create a free and independent justice department that would not be affected if prosecuting a highly networked politician, and the common people in everyday lives have to rise against people who create such an environment. What a shame for a country with such a rich history and that is the world's largest democracy to be saddled with these corrupt politicians who lack a constructive agenda for the country and are leading it to ruin. These selfish and greedy politicians are taking advantage of the huge defense spending allotted by the government for their own gain. Instead of investing in infrastructure projects, these crooks are taking millions in kickbacks in the name of economic liberalization and privatization of the country's infrastructure. Sometimes these culprits go to the extreme lengths of killing someone who threatens to expose their doings.

Politicians everywhere, including the developed world, do favors and deals, but it needs to be done with the highest ethical standards and with the priorities of the nation in mind—not for the sole purpose of the politician's gain.

After a bit of revolt from the people, the Indian government in its typical half-ass fashion gave its citizens the right to access and review non-confidential central or state government records through Public Information Officers who are appointed by the government. How is this going to help curb corruption? Although this is a good way of showing people that the government cares about corruption, it is not enough to curb it because it does not guarantee any action against offenders. Transparency is good, but the half-ass government and its half-ass attitude need to do much more to eradicate corruption to the core. As long as the government keeps up its half-ass attitude toward corruption, the country will keep suffering economically making it a "wannabe" country that will never reach its full potential. This land, which is amazing in some ways but disturbing in so many others, will be pitied by the rest of the world if it doesn't correct itself, move in the right direction, and not get mired in silly and useless distractions.

Chapter 4
Lets Go Domestic and Foreign

The United States is the last superpower, so its foreign policy is highly influential. India's influence on international scene has been growing due to its status as a regional power and a potential superpower. Even though India is a regional power, it has a long way to go to be a superpower.

With over 20 million people of Indian origin living and working abroad, one of the main roles of India's foreign policy is to ensure their welfare and well-being. As a developed country and superpower, the United States has a much bigger foreign policy agenda to create a more secure, democratic, and prosperous world for the benefit of the American people and the international community. That is one of the main reasons for its war in Afghanistan and in Iraq—to create stability by ending hostility and establishing a democratic government. The other end of its foreign policy also involves the nonproliferation of the nuclear technology to ensure and inhibit the creation of nuclear weapons.

India's history of collaboration with other countries goes a long way, but during cold war, India adopted a policy of not associating itself with any superpower, although it did develop close ties with the Soviet Union from which it received extensive military support. When the cold war ended, India strengthened its diplomatic and economic ties with the United States and many other countries, including the European Union. As India's governments changed, its military relationship turned from Russia to Israel and the United States for various reasons, including the best deals for military aid.

The cold war era was an intense military, political, and space race between the two superpowers, along with the race to seal deals with various countries on a number of programs. But after the collapse of Soviet Union, the relationship between the two countries changed. While the two superpowers wanted to create a firm relationship so they could work on fixing various international unstable regions, their disagreement leading up to the Kosovo war and Iraq war further undermined their desire to work together. The two powerful, mainstream societies had always had the common goal of curbing terrorism and establishing international stability, but various economic deals with other countries and Russia's authoritarian rule strained their relationship. The two countries should stop giving cold shoulders to each other because of each other's domestic or foreign policies and establish a strong partnership to make things work.

President Obama and Joe (and I don't mean Joe the plumber) Biden, who has extensive experience in foreign policy, are working very closely with and reaching out to all ranks of the Russian government to forge a successful partnership. This is in stark contrast to the Bush administration. While the Republican administration took an unilateral course in their foreign policy with no strategic partnerships other than willing participants, the tactical Obama administration is setting a cordial tone with Russia, emphasizing new cooperation on a number of issues and diplomatically resolving issues in Georgia and Ukraine. The Republican administration on the other hand not only did not pursue bilateral talks to resolve issues and strengthen relationships but continuously agitated the Russian administration by announcing plans to build an antiballistic missile defense system in Poland in response to Russia's aid to Iran's nuclear power program. Although the Republicans had good intentions of not hurting the good guys, these spontaneous but undiplomatic reactions could easily agitate the good guys. The Republicans badly needed an experienced and sound foreign relations leader instead of leaving this responsibility to an inexperienced Cheney. Both the Republican administration and the Russian administration continuously engaged themselves in cold war-like tactics that worked each other up during the invasion of Georgia and military cooperation in Venezuela and led to nothing but heated controversies.

Even though Russia and the United States had signed a treaty on strategic offensive reductions and an affirmation on a new relationship way back in 2002, the two parties never kept their promises on this declaration and continued to strain their association without making any attempts to resolve issues diplomatically. After the exhaustive years of war and tension under Bush and Cheney, an aggressive economic policy to give the domestic economy a boost and a balanced foreign policy to set things straight with the rest of the world from Obama and Biden has been a relief to everyone. It is right that the Obama administration initiated the "reset" to all the hostilities between Russia and the United States to enable a fresh start; the Russian administration should know that it is equally responsible to make this fresh relationship work.

Instead of debating who is failing the relationship, the two premier entities should share critical facts with each other that will help understand what is needed to make the relationship work and help alleviate the threat of a global confrontation. They should work together to reduce all dictators' and terrorists' negative influence on the mainstream society by collectively driving political and economic sanctions on them. As a display of good faith and international social responsibility, Russia should stop sending or aiding international arms dealers who are supplying weapons to unstable dictators, terrorists, drug traffickers, and criminals.

There are a lot of dictators running countries even though they are not capable of doing anything except exerting power and control. Lots of them are lurking on the continent of Africa, while a few of them are in the prowl in Asia and Europe. Some of these countries don't have constitutions, while others do but the leaders don't believe in following them and do what they feel. Why couldn't the United Nations (UN) and the United States finish the job during the Korean and the Vietnam Wars? It is understandable that international politics play a major role in wars, but what is the point in investing hundreds of billions of dollars in country's defense programs if the politicos involved in the military strategies can't get the job done? The world would have two less evildoers now if the UN and the United States had finished the job by bringing down the dictators and democratizing these two countries. The job to finish the communists in North Korea and Vietnam would have been easier if the Soviets and the Chinese were on the U.S. side. Regardless of trade and economic treaties between various countries, the permanent members of the UN should always stick together when it comes to military action against communists who blatantly and repeatedly break human rights rules. What is the point of having the UN and permanent membership if they all disagree on various military issues but cannot commit to one united military agenda? Although North Korea and Vietnam may not be a threat to the outside world, the governments and their people still carry a one-sided, abusive relationship, and the people don't see even a dim light at the end of the tunnel. Peace and stability are required in any country or region but not when it means having malicious dictators who ignore human rights and economic rules.

If actress and activist Jane Fonda were not so rebellious, feminist, and ignorant about the communist activities in Vietnam, she would not have traveled to Vietnam during the war in support of the communist regime. If Fonda were a Vietnamese citizen rooting for the Americans, she would have been killed instantly, without questions, by the communist regime if she were to return to Vietnam. Fonda and her fellow men and women in Hollywood have more freedom and face value than they realize and they should be a role model for U.S. citizens and the world, putting their foot on the right side of all just causes.

If Fonda claims to be a feminist, she should put all efforts to release Myanmar's opposition political leader Aung San Suu Kyi, who has been under house arrest since 1990, when her party won the country's general elections—something that did not stand well with the communist military leaders. What grown-up military leaders would curb a democratic leader who had come to power unless they are a twisted control freaks? The low-life dictatorial military junta in the country has continuously defied UN negotiations to release Kyi, and the only way to bring democracy to that country is to get rid of the male chauvinists in the military junta. For about two decades Kyi has been a Prime Minister elect while being under detention and all the international community has been doing is giver her various awards and prizes including the Nobel Peace Prize. The communists not only have her under detention but have been continuously killing protestors against the military. This has got to stop. If tough economic sanctions don't work against the junta, then military action definitely will. Democracy is the only way for people in that country to prosper. As usual, these good-for-nothing military rulers have created so much economic negligence and disruption that even after democracy is restored it will take years to rebuild that ravaged nation.

Why are the stupid communists allowed to break all the rules and put themselves in power? Even if that's the only way they can come to power anywhere, they should never be allowed to ruin any country. Too bad if the dumbshit communists can't win any fair general elections, even with an enormous amount of dumb luck. That's because they don't know how to play fair politics or run a government; they only know how to show power and control.

For the superpower, it's more about creating diplomatic atmosphere everywhere while taking advantage of talent and resources in a righteous way; for these dictatorial countries, it's always about controlling power. They believe that confronting the superpower on any issue and getting their way somehow makes them superior and better. The best solution for compliance from these countries would be to create a more aggressive UN body consisting of a number of countries that go after these dictatorial countries in a diplomatic way, with less interference from developed nations that creates a false impression of bias toward these dictators. But the solution is very complicated because for these dictators, compliance means giving in to a higher authority and that is the last thing they want to do even if it means jeopardizing the lives and careers of their citizens.

The main purpose of the UN and the United States is not to invade the countries with dictators but to safeguard the lives of the neighboring countries and sometimes the lives of the people in the country itself. History has taught us that these maniacal and egotistical dictators will do anything to safeguard the control they have on their people. The UN and the United States want to take every precautionary measure to make sure this does not happen again and have been in talks with North Korea (along with a number of European and Asian countries) to disarm its nuclear program.

For some clever whack jobs, like the Venezuelan president Hugo Chavez, it's less about confrontation and more about control. The constitution of his country was changed so that he could run for office forever and be in control until he dies. These irrational dictators who only want to safeguard their control on their country and have negligible interest in developing their country or upholding world peace only heighten the complexity of world peace and diplomacy. It has become a norm for dictators to use election to give the impression that the nation is democratic, but they rig the elections. These dictators are only looking for power and control and what better way to do it than to make its citizens as puppets forever? People in these countries at any cost should not allow these moronic dictators to change the constitution so they could run for elections as long as they want.

The United States enjoyed good political and economic relations with Cuba and Iran until revolutions in those countries in the mid and latter part of the twentieth century put anti-American dictators in power. Although the Cuban dictatorship did not encourage violence against American interests after the trade embargo, the Iranian religious dictatorship encouraged violence against American interests. Currently the only problem the United States has with Cuba is that it has a dictator and even though the country is peaceful, its economy has significantly deteriorated. A lot of Cuban Americans have been extremely angry and agitated over the years against the brutal dictator because of the country's economic decline. One could understand the anger of these Cuban Americans against the dictator since before he took over in a coup, the country's economy was stronger and more advanced than that of any Latin American or European country. Although President Obama eased some economic sanctions on Cuba to help improve its citizens' lives, he is very much aware that a trade embargo can only be lifted if it returns to democracy.

The two dictators claimed their hostility is due to America's arrogance and desire to be a global dictator, but President Obama said in his inaugural speech that they must not blame their societies' ills on the West. It is so true with the dictators and militants that they are trying to create ill will and hatred in their society against the developed countries by blaming all their problems on the developed countries. If the entire world were to be one perfect place with no violence and no forceful autocratic dictators, the United States wouldn't be spending billions of dollars forcing on wars while putting the lives of thousands of its own citizens in danger. As a free, stable, and democratic superpower, it always intends to and has taken the role of a big brother, along with the assistance from world governing bodies, to create free, stable, and democratic regions around the world that would help create a peaceful earth. That's in a perfect world; in reality these narcissistic dictators don't view diplomatic relations with the superpower as normal and not part of the negotiations but as being a superpower's puppet even if an embargo would mean the downfall of their country's economy.

And when these dictators are accused of doing something wrong, they do not want to accept responsibility. As President Obama clarified, the United States wants these countries to take their rightful place in the community of nations, but that's not going to happen unless these dictators accept real responsibilities and moves their countries toward moderate and progressive democracy. Talk is cheap and actions speak louder than words so these leaders should implement real changes in their countries. These countries need a democratic government that understands the true meaning of diplomatic relations and will always strive for the betterment of the country, with support from developed countries. These dictators need to understand that if they want their country to be better, they will need the support from developed countries and that doesn't mean becoming a puppet.

Conspiracy theorists have the dubious distinction of feeding the paranoid minds of these dictators with unscrupulous and baseless hypothesis of a new world order that the UN, the United States, and the Soviets are working toward, that is a totalitarian one-world government. These theories have fueled the suspicious minds of the dictators to gain even more power and control. Conspiracy theorists should shut the hell up, and the dictators should work toward transforming their countries into moderate democratic entities. Don't they get it? It's the social and economic powers and policies of the countries that represent them in the world order and these conspiracies are nothing but a way to throw the weak dictators off balance.

The United States, with an open-mind, wants to have diplomatic relations with every single country, whether developed or developing or underdeveloped, but resistance from close-minded dictators from these countries has caused tension between the United States and these countries. Take in the case of Taliban, which was the chaotic governing political party in Afghanistan in 2001. The United States tried everything to avoid confrontation with these unruly militants after the 9/11 attacks, but when Taliban refused to give bin Laden up, it had no other choice but to go to war with them. Although the United States spent billions of dollars on military and economic assistance to Afghanistan during the cold war, when it was fighting the Soviet Union, the United States had enough from these low-life criminals and had to launch an attack on the Taliban and Al-Qaeda. If Taliban members and the citizens of Afghanistan were a lot smarter, they would have given the militant leader up and avoided the deaths of a number of innocent civilians. As fate would have it, this already war-torn country, which is one of the poorest nations in the world, had no idea what was coming but this time would go through a war to build a democratic and stable government that is looking after the needs of its people.

Keeping in mind the attack that killed thousands of innocent civilians in the World Trade Center, the U.S. military routed and killed thousands of Taliban and Al-Qaeda operatives who were no match to the sophisticated U.S. military equipment. But the question still remains why hasn't the notorious bastard bin Laden, who has created havoc in the lives of everyone around him, been captured or killed? The U.S. military should end its occupation in

Iraq and then increase its presence in Afghanistan, so it can capture or kill all remaining Al-Qaeda and Taliban members and safely return home. The region needs stability and a stable government that can meet the needs of its impoverished citizens. The United States is trying to help, but at some point it must let their mainstream society evolve itself. The United States needs to stop pushing so hard for these underdeveloped people to change for the better and let them figure it out. The mainstream society is extremely passive, and the militants live in a parallel universe that can only be described as a fantasyland. Instead the United States needs to create a stronger government in these underdeveloped countries, so that they can take care of their citizens, both good and bad, in the right way.

The current governments in Afghanistan and Iraq are not very strong, and the U.S. military is the one taking care of the streets in those countries. The governments in these countries need to be stronger and take charge of the situation with tough positive ties with its people and an exceptionally tough law enforcement team. In an effort to get rid of the cowardly militants who always sought protection in between innocent citizens, the U.S. military would sometimes accidentally kill some of the innocent civilians, but the weak local governments would criticize them for their actions. These simplex-minded governments should instead play it in such a way that they don't portray the U.S. military as the bad guys, which they are not, and at the same time show sympathy toward the innocent families who have lost lives while denouncing the acts of cowardly militants who are just incapable of doing anything other than spreading violence. For the mainstream civilians of the nations of Afghanistan and Iraq, it has been a chicken and egg situation; they know they can have a better economy and country only with aid from allied forces but they want the allied forces to leave the country because the terrorists are instigating violence because of their presence. These civilians of the mainstream society in these countries should make up a firm mind to back their government, and the allied forces should commit themselves to build a better country and economy, while making every effort to bring the extremists to justice. Although there are casualties, the government with its positive propaganda should get the civilians on its side and ask them to help the government hand in militants who live among them. All these strategies will help put these cowardly militants away for good.

Hundreds of billions of dollars have already been spent on these two lingering wars, keeping only the oil and defense lobbyists happy. It's time for the government to stop spending money on these underdeveloped countries. These countries need to understand that the developed countries are always willing to help in anyway they can, but currently countries like the United States are doing it by undercutting their own domestic budgets. I would rather see the United States undercut foreign assistance and increase its domestic budget until the country's economy gets back on its feet and as the recession subsides; it can increase the foreign assistance as needed. If even after decades of foreign assistance to these underdeveloped countries, they can't get back on their feet, then they are either too dependent on foreign assistance or they are just hopelessly underdeveloped and no amount of foreign assistance is going to help. The amount of foreign assistance that the United States and other developed countries give to the developing and the underdeveloped world is immeasurable, and some of these countries will see the value in it only when it's gone.

It is not only the financial and military assistance that the United States provides to a number of foreign and developing countries, but it also ranges anywhere from free trade agreements (FTA) to providing counter-terrorism intelligence to a number of democratic countries. The United States has FTAs with about fourteen developed and developing countries. These have helped the countries to expand their economies tremendously and improve education, health services, and environmental programs.

It is time for India to put together some FTAs with developed nations, especially the European Union (EU) and the United States, but it has to significantly improve its infrastructure before it locks down any FTAs with these nations. Even though it started FTA talks with the EU in 2007, the domestic politics of the multiparty coalition government and lack of agreement from all parties on trade liberalization is holding India back. A progressive single-party government in India is vital to establish further trade liberalization and create multilateral agreements with the developed world that can take India to the next level. Indian citizens should elect an educated government with good leadership and negotiating skills that can see the necessities and advantages of building FTAs with the developed nations. The Indian government is usually slow in responding to complicated trade agreements that it cannot fathom, giving them simple historical numbers and explaining the advantages of a FTA between a developed and developing country should open their eyes in astonishment. Although governments have designed exchange programs to enhance trade relations between the two countries, with India lowering and eliminating tariffs on pharmaceutical and soft drink products, a comprehensive FTA would give a huge boost to the country's unplanned infrastructure development and retail sectors. It's simply impossible to step into a new economic era without FTAs, and it's absolutely ridiculous for critics to claim that a FTA between India and developed economies is impossible because of various complex intricacies of its economies.

The United States, on the other hand, even though a successful FTA promoter and implementer should consider removing tariffs and quotas in its textile and agriculture industries because this would tremendously help farmers and consumers in the developing countries. The United States and India (or any other developing country for that matter) should seriously push for FTA talks and lower tariffs that would not only grow the economy but also increase standards and efficiency in a number of sectors in developing nations. Vice President Joe Biden, who is an expert in U.S. foreign relations and policy, should sincerely and critically review U.S. FTAs to extend them to emerging markets in Asia that will thrust the world economy back into motion.

The United States provides strategic and effective assistance to any number of foreign countries to help them better their lives by supporting a number of programs, including human rights, poverty reduction, quality education, improved public health, and also to prevent and respond to conflict, which displays the superpower's amazing character around the world, especially when its own economy has been in a recession. What I certainly don't agree with is the fact that President Obama doubled the U.S. foreign assistance budget for the year 2010, even when states are slashing their yearly budgets and cutting a number of essential programs. Instead of doubling the U.S. foreign assistance budget, the United States should open up FTAs with the developing countries. The resulting economic growth in those countries should be used to set aside funds for their assistance programs. These strategies will not only help all the states keep their annual budgets and key programs but will also create independent developing countries that won't need direct economic assistance from the superpower.

The superpower also works with countries on postwar cleanup of light automatic weapons, rocket-propelled grenades, and landmines, which helps save lives and prevents these weapons in the wrong hands. It is not only the post-conflict weapons cleanup it gets involved in, but also, as a big brother, it helps these countries in social and economic recovery that's crucial to create internal and regional stability. But once that's done the little brothers should be left alone, so they can be independent, and the big brother can concentrate on furthering its own human development index.

The United States may have softened its outward stance on some of the non-threatening countries by easing some economic sanctions, but it still believes that every country's leadership should be elected democratically. A handshake with any dictator in front of the world media only means that the superpower still believes in keeping their friends close and their enemies even closer.

The superpower has been even more misunderstood in the very important international issue of weapons of mass destruction (WMD); it has been actively and diplomatically trying to resolve threats of proliferation through bilateral and multilateral talks. Although other developed countries have been supporting the superpower in diffusing the WMD danger posed by some dictators, these allies should take a more direct approach and spearhead some if not all of the bilateral and multilateral discussions. While other developed countries should be taking a more direct approach, the international governing bodies like the UN, NATO, andG8 should take more leadership roles, keeping a firm ground against these elements. All member countries of these international governing bodies should review their member selection process to ensure representatives to these bodies not only represent their countries fairly and strongly but also collectively stand against countries that do not abide by the international laws of peace and justice. On another level, these governing bodies should review their leadership selection process to ensure inclusion of individuals who would enhance and enrich the value of these governing bodies and also be ready to fairly and severely punish suspect nations for their wrongdoing. Politics and secretive bargaining among its members during the leadership selection process should be barred, and more importance should be given to a nominee's experience in prior leadership roles, their future vision, and proposed agenda as the head of the organization. These visions and agendas not only decide the future direction of a country on the international map, but the collective direction of the world as a whole. It only makes sense to do it all right and with the best intentions and approach when these governing bodies spend billions of dollars on a number of reformative programs. These committees and leaders would not only be required to work with the dictators to better the welfare of their countries but also work on other important issues like the nuclear nonproliferation treaties. It is the job of the committees and the leaders of these international governing bodies to convince countries of the advantages of signing the non-proliferation treaty, so they can use nuclear supplies to create energy rather than weapons. If these countries are not convinced of certain guidelines in the treaty, they should negotiate with the governing bodies and not just give up on the deal. The main concern of these governing bodies is to make sure these countries don't develop nuclear weapons, and they only want to constantly monitor the nuclear supplies and the nuclear energy plants.

For a country like India, surrounded by countries armed with nuclear weapons, it's imperative to work with the developed world and the governing bodies to make sure it would get the required security in case any of its neighbors attack. Being an economic leader and a progressive country in the region, it should work with the governing bodies, the developed world, and its nuclear-armed neighbors to bring the changes needed to create a nuclear arms safe region by collectively getting rid of them. Signing the nuclear treaty, along with FTAs with the United States and Europe, will not only immensely benefit everybody economically, politically, and strategically, but also will poise India to be recognized immediately as a permanent member of the UN Security Council, which will increase its clout among both developed and developing nations. This would also get a significant boost to India's infrastructure and manufacturing investment, resulting in a good competition with its neighbor China, who already has an advantage in both those entities giving them a price-point advantage.

Although most developed countries enjoy wonderful bilateral relations with their neighbors, a lot of developing countries are struggling to maintain normal relations with their neighbors because of a number of reasons. The United States has been enjoying spectacular relations with its immediate neighbors Canada and Mexico and provides military and financial help whenever needed. India has been struggling to maintain normal relations with its neighbors, which includes Pakistan, Sri Lanka, and Bangladesh. Even though

India has made significant efforts to improve relations with Pakistan, that country seems to have gone in the other direction by constantly crossing the border, instigating military battles, and not stopping terrorists who are trying to create havoc in India.

History has it that Romans conquered the home of Jews, called the Judas, and renamed it Palestine, which was later conquered by the Arabs who inhabited the land for about thousand years. Okay, so both Jews and Palestinians lived on this land at some point in time, but now that we live in a civilized society, why can't they coexist and live peacefully? Some people are so ignorant, envious, and hateful of powerful entities that they will try to do anything to bring them down. What these ill-bred rebels don't know is that their hatred is only paving a clearer path to their self-destruction. Arabs and Jews have fought four wars in this region but have only come so close to resolutions mainly because of the fanatic attitude of the rebels. Even after Israel twice offered over 90 percent of West Bank, Gaza, East Jerusalem, and a significant portion of Jewish settlements, the Palestine Liberation Organization (PLO) chairman Yasser Arafat turned down the offers. With a straight poker face, he even signed a declaration renouncing violence and recognizing the right of Israel to exist.

Why did Chairman Arafat reject the offer? It wasn't Arafat's ego or lack of diplomatic skills or lack of negotiation strategies that made him reject the best ever deal offers by Israel. While he started off the struggle for a Palestinian state with Israel on a square note, greed got the better of him once aid money started pouring in from the developed world, including from Israel. Arafat diverted over a billion dollars of aid money into his personal account, some of which he used to support the militants and the rest were invested in various interests all over the world, while he made the poor Palestinian people suffer. Due to his greediness, he continually became a deterrent to the peace process, so he could keep building his portfolio without any consideration for his people. This is the state of mind of all the leaders of underdeveloped countries who start off their fight all for their people, but at some point lose sight of their original goal and end up neglecting the needs of the people. There are very few to no leaders in underdeveloped countries who consistently stick to the agenda of developing the country to reach the goal they started with.

Palestinians and Arabs who keep proclaiming the destruction of Israel should understand that Romans and Arabs grabbed the land of Palestine from Jews about a thousand years ago, and even when Israel is ready to give most of the Palestine land back to them, the leadership of Palestine and its homegrown militants are acting childish and immature by not taking any kind of deal. Instead, the leaders at the top in Palestine are taking advantage of the aid money to fill their pockets, while spreading hatred among its citizens to keep the struggle alive so the aid money keeps pouring in. Fighting for land with violence between two groups was done during the reigns of kingdoms in history and in this technology-centric civilized and educated era, minds must be transformed enough to resolve issues diplomatically. The Israeli government and a number of other prominent world leaders tried to recognize another Palestinian leader who was not as hard-headed as Arafat, so they could discuss and resolve various issues. It seemed to Palestinians, especially Arafat, that it was not about establishing a Palestinian state but more of silly and aimless power struggle that was not going to take them anywhere.

The corrupt and inept Palestinian militant group Hamas has already shown that having a rebellious attitude and animalistic fighting instincts does not help you run a government, as they failed miserably after winning the elections. The militants need to understand that if they keep fighting, that's all they will be doing for the rest of their lives, while the rest of the mainstream world will keep moving forward. There is no point in killing each other for no reason as both Jews and Palestinians have equal rights to the land they inhabit right now; it is considered best for Palestinians to give up any kind of struggle and move on with their constructive lives. The Palestinians instead should take the deal from Israel and rebuild a moderate society, with a strong political and economic foundation, creating another example of a peaceful, stable, moderate, and prosperous society. Harboring negative feelings about others only leads to destruction, and in a civilized society that we all have formed, positive feelings lead to great results that take us to great heights.

The fact remains that Jews once populated the land that's now Israel, and Palestine was a land that once belonged to Israel. So the leaders of Middle East should stop questioning the existence of Israel and work on a compromise that will allow for the coexistence of two diverse cultures. The leaders of the Arab world should also understand that even though Israel is powerful in many perspectives, it is a stable country that would not attack its neighbors unless provoked. The militants should give up their violent tactics, so that the two sides can agree on a common roadmap for peace that will result in a secure Israel and a peaceful democratic Palestine. Even though the United States has ties with Israel, it wants an unbiased and peaceful resolution to the whole Israel-Palestine conflict, so it can bring more political and economic stability to the entire region.

The Arab world, instead of being passive-aggressive to all the issues including financial support to the Palestinian government, should actively work with the rest of the world to resolve their issues diplomatically. This also involves denouncing and dismantling all terrorist organizations that are in their countries and actively supported by their local governments. Administrations in the developed world will change term after term, but the core domestic and foreign policies never change and that includes not actively engaging or encouraging any domestic or foreign organizations that promote violence in various parts of the world. When looking from a third-party's unbiased point of view, it is clear that dismantling these violent organizations requires a change in mindset of their people. The developing minds should stop interpreting this as a way for the developed world to treat the developing world as their puppets. The idea of the developed world is to resolve all issues diplomatically and promote democracy all over the world. The governments in the Middle East should stop encouraging the militia and develop a government military to defend their nations instead. Israel should stop building settlements in controversial lands and return the land to Palestinians. The Palestinians should elect a strong, progressive, and democratic government that does not include the militia, as they only know how to fight constantly and not run a government; this is so important for the prosperity of Palestinian people. While the religious leaders on both sides may have various notions about the land each of them should control, the conflict should be resolved in a political and practical way by an unbiased and fair third party.

The United States did the right thing by going to war in Afghanistan against Taliban and Al-Qaeda because the twisted religious fanatics brought it on themselves on September 11, 2001 by killing thousands of people in New York and Washington, D.C. Military action was unavoidable as that was the only right response for the militants' actions. It's not about power or ego or who's better but about teaching the uneducated, deranged, and immature militants to grow up. All planes were hijacked by a score of young terrorists who seemed to have been brainwashed by people who want to push their own selfish agenda. At the end of the day, what did the terrorists achieve? Nothing but the killing of thousands of innocent people, destroyed thousands of families, jobs, and showed the world what they hold in their small, negative minds. These young, vulnerable, stupid terrorists are being told that if they kill as many *infidels* as possible, they will attain *martyrdom*, get seventy-two virgins, and their families will be taken care of forever. Who in their right mind would believe this teaching? People who have been fed to believe in hatred toward infidels or a sex-starved kid eagerly looking forward to getting laid with seventy-two virgins?

Although one cannot put a price on the innocent lives lost in the World Trade Center (WTC) attack, the economic damage was over eighty billion dollars. All because some opium-shooting, deranged morons living in caves in Afghanistan thought they could play with more virgins if they killed innocent people in America. These extremists who engage in violence are the scum of the earth that the mainstream society needs to eradicate. The 9/11 hijackers were no religious martyrs but twisted scumbags who drank alcohol, paid for lap dancers and sex escorts, used sex toys, and watched pornographic videos while jerking off next to their holy book. These good-for-nothing militant leaders handsomely paid the good-for-nothing-hijackers' families, calling the hijackers martyrs for the deed, while the mainstream society calls them below-average idiots who were paid to commit a gruesome mass murder-suicide. These young people are wasting their lives for someone else's disturbing agenda that will take them nowhere. The real martyrs on the plane were the passengers who stormed into the cockpit and tried to tussle the hijackers to the ground.

After they were successful in destroying the WTC and killing thousands of people, the Taliban and Al-Qaeda felt like an underdog team winning a championship. But when the rest of the mainstream world was horrified at the destruction and the U.S. bombs hit the caves where they were hiding, the radicals must have understood what sore losers they were. The Taliban and Al-Qaeda have no real power whether in terms of intelligence or politics. If they did they would have built a strong and stable government, as well as an economy in Afghanistan instead of producing drugs and insinuating violence.

Regardless of whether foreign policies or counter-terrorism policies have been written for these extreme terrorist behaviors, they need to be treated the way they treat the mainstream society—with ignorance and disrespect. While these radicals believe that through dramatic violence they can instill fear in mainstream society, it is having the opposite effect of making the mainstream society even stronger. Even before 9/11, the FBI and CIA had massive counter-terrorism efforts that included collecting intelligence to avert any tragedy and criminal investigations after the fact. But the entities became so big and so did their egos and bureaucracy. The FBI and CIA should reduce the bureaucratic chaos, so they can easily work with other government intelligence teams to ensure there's no future damage by these extremists in the developed world or to any mainstream moderate society. Since these intelligence and investigative organizations have grown too big, the federal government needs to review the structure of the entire safety and security entities under its leadership, so it can organize and strategize intelligence gathering in a more efficient manner. There should be a secure international counter-terrorism intelligence database created that can be accessed by all trusted developed and developing governments. Sharing intelligence on international terrorists and their plots would help avert disasters. Along with the database, extensive partnerships with all intelligence gathering communities between trust-worthy developed and developing governments should be created that would not only make information sharing easier but also help reduce the high cost for these complex and extensive undertakings by eliminating redundant resources. This database should not be shared with governments who promote extremist groups or have shady relationships with them because these governments and entities would only be spying to find out what plots have been uncovered. The FBI and the CIA should only work on very high-priority cases involving counter-terrorism and other cases, so they can free up resources from other less important issues.

Apart from its ties with Israel, the United States also maintains a special relationship with Saudi Arabia that dates back to World War II, when the United States provided military training to help the Saudis defend their abundant natural resources. A number of U.S. presidents have provided reassurances to Saudi Arabia that it will help it defend its territorial integrity because of the volatility in the region by providing military equipment and training. The United States-Saudi relationship though smooth had its occasional strains due to strong U.S. ties with Israel. Saudi Arabia was dead against the 1948 establishment of Israel in the former Arab-dominated Palestine territory and was concerned with the United States providing biased support to Israel to drive the Palestinians away. Saudi Arabia has been a little unhappy about the U.S. stance on Israel-Palestine conflict, but it has to realize that the United States only wants to defend Israel's right to exist, peacefully, as a nation.

While the United States takes a tough approach to counter-terrorism, its special ally in the Middle East has taken a soft approach to Saudi citizens who were previously convicted of trying to follow bin Laden's steps in Afghanistan. Although some critics claim that these hard-core criminals don't usually listen to any soft approaches, the Saudi kingdom has already noticed close to 90 percent success rate. The rehab program also involves extensive educational training, religious and psychological counseling, and broad mainstream social network support that will help them ease into the society that they slipped away from a long time ago. A 90 percent success rate indicates that through careful psychological training, the human mind can adopt a second alternative option while completely erasing the previous option that led them nowhere. These programs clearly show that a combination of a simplex mind, a lost soul, extreme anger, and passion can be easily taken advantage of by fanatics who are greedy and battling a lost cause. This soft approach may not work in other democratic countries and may need to be tested; hard approaches are a sure way of successfully dealing with hard-core terrorists in democratic countries.

Some question why Saudi Arabia is assisting in the crackdown and rehabilitation of Saudi terrorists when employees of their government helped some of the 9/11 hijackers, the answer is that the Saudi government unknowingly lent a hand to its citizens who turned out to defame the kingdom, and the Saudi government feels guilty. The progressive and business-oriented Saudi kingdom is ashamed of the actions of their people and is trying to make amends to their image by keeping its citizens in check. The moderate Saudi government is completely aware that any extremism by its citizens in the name of a twisted faith that does not exist in any holy book will only tarnish their brand that exudes luxury and attracts millions of tourists to their country. Even a hint of extremism from the Saudi government and its citizens in the future will only harm its oil and tourism. To keep both the religiously devout but not radicals and the progressive community in their country content and satisfied, the Saudi government and most other progressive business-oriented kingdoms in the Middle East have divided their land, so the not-so-religious can still entertain themselves outside the boundaries of the religious laws.

A lot of people living in developing countries are scared of the mafia and the underworld because of their reckless behavior toward innocent citizens. Existence of Mafia in developed countries in the twenty-first century is very rare and quickly subdued once detected. Murders, robberies, and aggravated assaults have been most prevalent among the developed world, including the United States. The government can't stop these crimes because individuals commit them spontaneously. In the United States organized and unorganized crimes existed in the early 1900s, but today the alarming rate of unorganized crimes has everyone take note of the nation's loose regulations on gun possession. It is alarming to see that people are thronging to gun stores and gun shows now that President Obama is looking to ban assault rifles. The National Rifles Association (NRA) is so selfishly opposing this ban that they are encouraging people, including students, to own guns. It claims attacks in schools and colleges can be avoided if every student owns a gun. Have these NRA members gone mad? Everybody has the right to be selfish to a certain extent, but come on this association has gone one step too far in furthering their interests and business. If every student on the campus owned a gun, every single stupid fight on campus would end up in a deadly gunfight. It's disgusting that these NRA members are only interested in selling guns and not in the safety of the community. President Obama should not give in to the gun lobbyists and ban assault rifles immediately, so nobody, whether sane or insane, is able to purchase these deadly weapons by taking advantage of this loophole.

These assault rifles are also ending up in the hands of Mexican drug cartels in the United States and Mexico that are terrorizing the people and the governments. Gun culture has been popular in the United States since the Revolutionary War, and its time to make this culture unpopular by banning the public from having these weapons. The gun lobbyists have spent way too much on furthering their deadly agenda and it's time to give them a break by banning both the lobbyists and weapons. It doesn't matter whether innocent people are losing their lives here in the United States or in Mexico—a life lost is a life lost regardless. It is so pathetic that the NRA and its lobbyists are displaying their cold shoulders even after they know that the Mexican drug cartel network here in the United States is paying cash to buy easily accessible high-powered weapons to destroy any opposition in Mexico, which is devastating to the already economically struggling country. The FBI, the CIA, and the ATF, along with the NRA, should upgrade the customer-list network so that it doesn't take several months to find out somebody went to different licensed gun dealer everyday to buy high-powered weapons to smuggle across the border. The gun dealers should have instant access to a database to know if a customer is buying very large quantities of high-powered weapons so they can alert authorities to take action instantly. The U.S. government should seriously consider creating a national customer database or gun registry that can be instantly accessed by every single gun dealer in the country and not rely on a paper trail. The gun regulations in the southern states near the Mexican border should be tightened and vehicle checks for guns and ammunition crossing the border to Mexico should be increased.

It only shows their greediness when some NRA members and gun dealers argue that if banning and tight gun regulations happen in the United States, the Mexican drug cartels will go somewhere else to purchase the firearms. The NRA members and the gun dealers have a who-cares-if-we-are-doing-the-right-thing mentality, but one can be certain the NRA members' or the gun dealers' views would change in an instant if any of their close family members were killed by one of these weapons smuggled by the drug cartels. Even if the second amendment gives citizens the right to bear arms to defend themselves, it is time to change the law since vast majority of the weapons owned are used in crimes to kill people and not for self-defense.

In India, the entire underworld gangs own imported illegal firearms and only a small number of citizens own legal firearms because of its draconian antigun legislation that was mostly written during the British rule. It is the conservative nature of the mainstream Indian society that makes them not to own guns similar to the types who shun away from consuming alcohol. Indian government should not lift the ban on firearms import, as it would be hard for the law enforcement to keep up with the violence that would ensue in addition to the already existing non-violent chaos.

It all started in Sicily during the ninth century when Sicilians took refuge in the surrounding hills and formed a secret society called the Mafia to unite the native Sicilians. In the United States, many Mafia members befriended many actors/actresses, extorted movie studio owners, and were involved in starting a number of casino/hotel businesses in Las Vegas. Extortion of movie bigwigs and illegal gambling are happening now in India, which indicates how far that country is from becoming a fully developed nation. Although the American Mafia has subsided and become more institutionalized, there are still a number of gangs active in the United States, and the government has an active gang-control unit to make sure all these gangs are kept under control. These violent gangs are active in schools, urban areas, and impoverished neighborhoods across the nation. When the mafia and the gangs get out of control, the FBI undercover agents usually infiltrate the mafia and gangs and gather enough information on the group's illegal activities. They break the group down by catching them by surprise and arresting all involved.

Society can take various approaches to stop people from starting and joining gangs by attending to people's reasoning for starting or joining gangs. Tending to the basic psychology and needs of people will help stop youths from starting and running gangs and will create a more stable society in the long term. Youths form gangs because they experience a sense of alienation and powerlessness or they experience lack of identity or lack of power and control, which could easily lead to frustration and anger resulting in violence. Providing various experiences for youths in schools that give them a sense of belonging or sense of power, control, and identity will greatly reduce formation of gangs in schools and effectively harness their strengths that may one day help them in their career. For troubled youths who are not in schools, the same experiences should be provided through establishments with which the youths are associated.

There are still a huge number of Mexican and Colombian cartels that control the distribution and sale of narcotics in the United States. The U.S. authorities are actively working with the Mexican and Colombian governments to curb these cartels, and they can only be curtailed by use of force and power, but these governments need to take immediate and extensive action to make the cartels history. Although Bush was ineffective on this issue, Obama is already taking action by creating a stronger border patrol group, so that the cartels don't infiltrate into the country. With the Mexican government already standing tough on these drug cartels in Mexico, they have started infiltrating the border towns in the United States creating havoc among the local residents. As these cartels will do anything to keep their lucrative business going, the U.S. government needs to push these cartels back into Mexico.

Organized crime is negligible in developed countries due to the strong government presence and a tough police force. People involved are brought to justice immediately. One doesn't hear about the Mafia on a day-to-day basis in developed countries, but you hear it everyday in developing countries like India, Mexico, and Colombia. On the other hand, a developed country like the United States is home to an increasing number of unorganized crimes that take a toll in terms of lives lost and money spent. About 1 percent of the adult population is behind bars—the highest percentage for any developed or developing country. Although violent and property crimes in the United States dropped to their lowest levels in 2005, it still costs the country over $500 billion a year for the criminal justice system, for private protection, loss of life and work, stolen goods and fraud, drug abuse, and drunk driving. When violent and property crimes were at a peak in the 1990s, the government took action to bring the crime rate down by putting more police on the streets, focused on serious, habitual offenders, and developed community programs that deter crime. The first seven years of the twenty-first century saw over 100,000 deaths due to unorganized crimes—close to triple that of any other developed country.

Because of the gun culture in the country, it has been a debate for several decades to enforce stricter firearm laws, including extensive background check and minimum age requirement to possess a firearm. This loose firearm law means many teenagers in impoverished neighborhoods carry guns, and shoot and kill people for either drugs, money, or sometimes no reason. There have been a number of killings on high school and college campuses across the United States, and it is alarming to see how easily these kids got hold of the firearms used for these heinous acts. Most of these kids are frustrated in life for some reason and easy access to guns is one way of venting their frustrations. So if the government were to enforce strict firearm laws, the kids would have to vent their frustrations in a different and hopefully positive way. It is also the responsibility of the family to keep their kids away from violence, drugs, and guns, so they can have a cleaner and healthier environment. If guns are to be used by kids, it has to be in a controlled environment during hunting season or at a shooting range; access to gun, whether at home or anywhere else, has to be avoided at any cost.

It is ironic that in a developed country like the United States one can see the best of the best talents and the worst of the worst. If the government and the people put forth more effort, they can change the worst of the worst into the best of the best, and that will have a marvelous effect in this already superb country and also on the rest of the world.

In developing countries like India, underworld mafia and politics go hand in hand, and that is one of the reasons government is not as strong as in a developed country. An educated, extraordinary government is required to end the nexus between the two. Organized crime is rampant in developing countries, and their connection with political figures and police, and their international reach have made it difficult for the government to bring all people involved to justice. How on earth could one imagine mafia successfully taking advantage of others in a big way without consequences unless the government had some kind of involvement in it? Initially, the underworld kingpins made money supplying drugs and arms to the citizens. And once they got a strong foothold, they got into extorting money for protection from wealthy businessmen. Over a period of time the mafia dons, with their scare tactics, knew they could do anything, so they channeled all the money into Bollywood (Indian equivalent of Hollywood) movie making and real estate development. Subsequently the quality of Indian movies went down, and real estate development projects under the mafia were shabby because they only were looking to make a quick buck. They forcefully hired directors, actors, actresses, and builders to perform according to their script in both industries and killed or attempted to kill anyone who did not adhere to their forceful tactics.

Mexican drug cartels are up to the same tricks in response to pressure from the government. Governments in developing countries should not take the approach that if you can't stop them, join them because that leads to self-destruction. The media and the general public are so enamored of organized crime bosses that lot of people get into this lifestyle for its grandeur and as a way to make some quick money not thinking of the risks involved. These dons go hand in hand with political figures, and they help each other without regard for their country. Each and every city has its don controlling his territory and connected to other dons and local political figures who get protection and money from the dons and return the favor by giving business deals to them.

Organized crime in India particularly in the city of Bombay goes back to 1940s, when Karim Lala set up gambling and bootleg liquor dens. The Bombay underworld during those times got a huge boost from the socialist regimes that put restrictions on the Indian economy. The collapse of the textile industry in the 1980s, which left many workers out of work, furthered the underworld crime organizations. Dawood Ibrahim has been named a global terrorist by the United States for his links with Al-Qaeda and its sister groups, and is presumed to be living a lavish and secluded life in Pakistan under the cover of ISI (Pakistan's intelligence agency). Only in a developing or underdeveloped country could a thug and a terrorist like Dawood Ibrahim, who is currently wanted by both Interpol and Indian government for funding Al-Qaeda and the 1993 bomb blasts in Bombay that left 250 people dead, would be able to have a deep-rooted nexus with the government. He has built a huge business empire there that is both legitimate and illegitimate, has made huge investments in Karachi real estate, is a major player in parallel credit system business, and the usual gold and drug smuggling. He helped President Musharraf in the recent elections to the extent that when visiting India Musharraf completely denied that Dawood is in Pakistan. Interpol and the CIA should use the aid money provided to Pakistan government to lure this scumbag to surrender; that will help cut financing to many terrorist organizations. Dawood Ibrahim's underworld rival Chotta Rajan, even though not involved with any terrorist organizations, has been evading capture due to his connections to many governments and law enforcement.

Mexico is one of the most beautiful developing countries; its beautiful beaches are top coastal vacation spots that attract about twenty million tourists a year, making it the eighth most visited country in the world. A totally different world from these beautiful vacation spots exists in the Mexico drug world, where drug cartels fight to retain their territory in drug trade that is estimated to be worth more than $20 billion a year. When Felipe Calderon took over as president of Mexico in December 2006, he vowed to put an end to all Mexican drug cartels and take over all parts of the country, especially in the northern states bordering the United States, where these cartels have been operating for years. For this task, he deployed more than 30,000 Mexican Army Special Forces and federal police forces in all the cartel territories, and the cartels have pushed back with violent confrontations that resulted in the deaths of over 4,000 people. The cartels have also killed a number of journalists who have written about their dirty laundry.

Calderon's mission is to regain control of the cartel territory, establish peace where the cartels have sown terror, and to rebuild judicial institutions by eliminating corruption that has infected local police departments. The cartels have upped their rebellion against the government to maintain the turf by increasingly going after the top federal law enforcement structure. A lot of arms, including machine guns and grenade launchers, that the cartels have been using in their attack are believed to be smuggled into Mexico from the United States, and Calderon wants to curb the supply of these arms to the cartels. Breaking years of secret operation, the drug cartels have started to battle it out in public with a daring hit list of law enforcement officials and threats on banners and graffiti on streets. The banners ask army soldiers to desert the military and join the cartels; some banners threaten those who get in the way of trafficking. If there was even a slightest hint of any of these events happening in the United States, these drug cartels would be routed within days and nobody would remember they existed.

Its high time United States increased help to its southern neighbor, so Calderon can make it a wonderful nation for its citizens. U.S. intelligence officials, along with their Mexican counterparts, should work together to apprehend these drug kingpins. Instead of installing a wall along the U.S.-Mexico border that would help in national security and curb drug trafficking, the U.S. government should go on a direct offensive against these cartels by sending its military force to Mexico. A taste of the military power to these below-average drug cartels will bring them down to earth and help the lives of innocent civilians. Military retaliation is the right response to these thugs since the cartels have been hiring a group of former Mexican military sharpshooters called los Zetas to do their dirty work. It is not that the drug cartels are more powerful than the government military, but they are brazen and fearless. The cartels and their families should be treated the same way they treat the families of innocent civilians because the cartels are not only drug pushers but also heavy drug users. They didn't think twice when they killed the daughter of a grieving mother who took out a front-page ad in a local newspaper because the cartel killed two of her innocent sons. These cartels are seriously out of their minds because they thought the front-page ad of a grieving mother was bad publicity to the cartel. The military shouldn't think twice to kill the cartels and their families because the cartel had no problem when they attempted to kill the editor of the newspaper that ran the story of the grieving mother. These cartels are just cowards because otherwise they wouldn't be running around with their heads up their butts.

As the CIA's cyber crime unit is trying to find out how to successfully stop the online Nigerian scam, another issue that's taken on giant proportions recently is the attack on ships by Somali pirates. Without a central government, more than 70 percent of the country's population living under the poverty line, and millions dependent on UN food aid, some citizens have turned to piracy. Although these pirates are small-time crooks, it is tough to stop them in action since they attack ships in the vast Indian Ocean. As the pirates have successfully sought hundreds of millions of dollars in ransom from the companies who own the captured ships, the French and the U.S governments have taken a tough approach toward bringing them to justice. But as history has taught us, people who do the right thing always win, and if these punk pirates are bold enough to attack ships and kill crews, as a long-term approach, the UN should bring down the militia in Somalia.

As the lawlessness spreads in this impoverished and undernourished continent, governments from various countries are trying to grapple with this new problem and find solutions. First, all assets of these pirates should be frozen so they don't have funds to carry out future attacks. Second, the UN and NATO should create a naval build up in the Somali gulf, around the Somali coast, and in international waters of the Indian Ocean to curtail future pirate attacks or to use force to end any pirate attack and free hostages. Third, the UN and NATO should successfully negotiate to release hundreds of hostages that are currently under the Somali pirates without paying a penny in ransom. Finally, a long-term approach to create a stable Somalia government that can take control of the chaotic situation should be taken. Shipping companies that use that route should not give in to these pirates. It's not about the money, but in the big picture, the pirates need to be taught a lesson that they can't rob people. Although one also feels pity for them since in a strange way they seem to be calling for help for their country to make it better.

Chapter 5
International Governors...Are They Really?

The international governing bodies like the UN, Group of 8 (G8), and the Group of 77 (G77) were created to act as a platform to discuss issues and promote joint, mutually beneficial programs. Unfortunately, they are becoming increasingly passive. One can't be passive and expect to make a huge difference in the lives of civilians of various countries. The G77, part of the UN, was created when member states categorized as developing nations realized they needed a common platform to discuss their economic issues, interests, and promote their collective developmental benefits. In other words, the developing nation members of the UN felt like their distributed agenda was being ignored for some reason and hence decided to form a separate group where they could form a unified agenda that they could take to the UN to be heard.

A decade after G77 was formed and right after the oil crisis and the global recession in the early 1970s, the developed world's eight major economic powerhouses felt the increasing need to create an informal forum to discuss social, political, and economic issues that affect the developed world. Instead of creating a strong working administrative structure, the G8 has introduced another loosely based G8+5 summit, adding the five countries from the emerging markets. The introduction of the five countries from the emerging markets would be a complete waste of time to debate on social, political, and economic issues in a forum that has a loosely based structure when the topics are relevant to the developed world but are often ignored in the emerging markets. The developing countries and emerging markets need forums that debate and assign tasks to members who can be held accountable to successfully resolving issues; that will not be done in existing G8+5 forums. Many of the issues discussed in this forum are totally valid and exist in the emerging markets, but they get ignored because of lack of funds and priority given to other important and critical issues existing in those countries.

The UN aims to act as a platform for its 192 member countries considering various issues like international law, international security, social/ economic development, and human rights. Of late the UN seems to have lost its touch, and the secretary general desperately needs to step up to the plate to redeem the organization as a formidable force in the international community. The UN was founded as a successor to the League of Nations, but it has continued the League's legacy of ineffectiveness as a poorly formed entity.

While the UN debates global issues that need to be resolved or eradicated, the G8+5 huddles together once in a while to discuss a range of topics that are important to the developed world and to create an example of the importance of these issues to the emerging markets. Members of the five countries that are considered the emerging markets should carefully listen to discussions by the members of G8 on topics like health, labor, energy, environment, and terrorism because these issues will become important to them in the future.

The UN and the G77 should expand their scope to actively look into international issues like presidential elections in dictatorial countries so that free and fair elections are conducted. Any misappropriation in these countries should be handled in the International Court of Justice and violation should result in severe political and economic sanctions. What is the point of having international governors if they are not able to actively participate in stopping any misuse of power by any country? When substantial presidential election fraud was reported in Iran, citizens of that country took their protests to the streets and a number of protestors were killed to silence them, rest of the world just looked on in horror. No leaders or international governors said or did anything about it. The lack of a reaction from the UN secretary general to all the developments in Iran was disappointing, especially when the media did not demand any reaction from the Secretary General, undermining the credibility of the international governing leader. During the election dispute, the attention-seeking Iranian president, whom Jay Leno correctly mispronounces as "I am a nut job", quietly sat in comforts waiting for the protests to calm down either with force or time—definitely not the sign of a good democratic leader but of a bad autocratic want-to-be leader.

While the Republican leaders in the United States complained about President Obama's passive stance on the issue, no leaders complained about the passive stance of the leaders of the international governors who should be actively protesting the fraud by the government to keep the conservative good-for-nothing dictator in power. Establishing strong international governors and instilling strong international governing leaders who openly chastise these unruly dictatorial leaders for their behavior and take appropriate action can ensure the safety and growth of the people. The international community collectively should work toward creating a more effective structure for all international governing bodies at all levels and should take extra care in electing not only effective and efficient leaders but also outspoken leaders for these entities. Credibility of the international governing body should be upheld on every occasion and strong verbal reactions should be given when jokers like Libyan dictator Qaddafi proposed dissolving a developed country like Switzerland and merging it into neighboring countries. The UN should create a strong example by kicking idiots like Qaddafi out of the UN for making such stupid remarks on a platform that is used to resolve serious international issues and conflicts.

To make a more credible workplace for its employees, the UN should reduce the pay scale and benefits, and add a bonus that is tied to workplace achievements. This would include the secretary general who doesn't deserve a salary of $200,000 if his achievements are not up to par for an international governing body leader. Since 85 percent of the UN's budget comes from voluntary contributions of the developed world, it is in their best interest for them to step up and provide input in all matters—operating and core mission agendas. The UN core mission budget for maintaining peace and security should come as much as possible from the governments where UN peace missions are being conducted. The UN operating budget, which runs in the billions of dollars and is the same as its core mission budget, is a little over the top considering that its political, diplomatic, and lending strategies have not been as effective as its peacekeeping missions. The UN should either decrease its operating budget by cutting expenses to match its effectiveness or increase its effectiveness to match its operating budget, which can be done by replacing its operating team with highly effective people. Members who make significant contributions in terms of game-changing ideas and processes should be held with higher regard than members who don't make any contributions.

The first G77 review found that the economic growth of developing countries had slowed but growth in the developed world had increased. Reviews and studies should be conducted to find out not only why growth slowed but also how the developing world can keep apace with the developed world. Also the share of total world exports of the developing countries declined compared to the increase in share by the developed countries. Again the whys and hows behind such numbers should always be investigated.

To make it more efficient, the G8+5 should be put under the arm of the UN similar to the G77 but all members should meet more often to confront and resolve more issues that regularly affect both the developed and developing worlds. If the UN has grown too big for it to work in a smooth and efficient manner, instead of having children organizations, the UN should be divided into chapters that would consist of a mixture of equal number of developed and developing countries and would handle specific issues. This would not only enable the developing countries to easily follow clear-cut examples from their developed counterparts but will help the developed nations easily manage and lead. These chapters of the UN will not only help the countries to manage issues easily but will help manage costs better by eliminating all the children organizations. These chapters should interchange the country memberships every decade or two, so they get to experience the dynamic vision of various leaders. Creating various UN chapters will help address and resolve issues more quickly. Splitting of the UN into a number of chapters would encourage faster and more effective development of individual countries. The current top UN structure would be retained to oversee the progress of each chapter. Creating various chapters of the UN will also decrease the failure rate of peacekeeping actions because member countries won't easily fail to reach consensus.

The UN's working structure is very ineffective and inefficient when it comes to responding to critical issues of violence and war. Not only do the members need to meet more often to debate critical issues and respond to them in a timely manner, they also need to have a mindset that is independent of their country. The efforts for economic development require the governing body member representing that country to be in tune with the economic needs of the nation. All these efforts necessitate a balanced, unbiased approach from its members that can only be achieved if members act as representatives of the governing body not as liaisons between the governing body and their country. The complexities involved in the working of these international governing bodies make it hard for the members to work on resolving tough issues; therefore the governing bodies should be located on independent islands where the members reside full time without being interrupted by any country's politics.

The UN General Assembly holds regular yearly sessions that run from September to December have become another social networking event that could be easily done from Myspace or Facebook and be more effective. What is the point of having special sessions of the General Assembly if the Security Council can't make the decisions? Despite the regular and special sessions meeting by the UN members, they have not been able to put on the table even a single alternative working strategy for the existing economic/ humanitarian aid to countries like Cuba, North Korea, and some African countries with useless dictators. The economic/humanitarian aid only helps the dictators and not the people. The UN should create a separate team that is completely dedicated to coming up with strategies to solve the issues of dictatorial and underdeveloped countries that are favorable to the citizens of those countries. The International Monetary Fund (IMF) and the World Bank should stop the ineffective strategies of throwing money away at these corrupt, good-for-nothing dictators and build strategies to transform these nations into working democracies. The UN, IMF, and the World Bank should stop appeasing these corrupt dictators in the hope that one day they will change these countries into democracies and instead take proactive actions to stop the cruelties of the dictators.

The IMF and the World Bank are at fault for their current reckless lending to corrupt dictators when they know the loans are not properly used and repayment is in question. Giving loans to underdeveloped governments that don't use the money to develop the country will only result in poverty traps for those governments, as they wouldn't be able to repay it for a very long time.

The shortfall in their revenue can be blamed on their irresponsible lending to fraudsters, and they can overcome it only by going back to their early years when all loan applications were carefully screened before approval. For this to be enforced, these lenders would need to clean their houses because loans are offered to corrupt dictators in return for kickbacks to the loan officers. Just as a number of American mortgage lenders went bankrupt because of their reckless lending to unqualified applicants, these international lenders will go down because of their negligence unless they take preemptive measures.

Before enforcing international sanctions or authorizing military action, the Security Council needs to investigate the situation and recommend procedures for peaceful resolution. If a dispute is beyond peaceful resolution, the Security Council needs to agree on enforcing partial or complete sanctions on the country responsible for the dispute. If sanctions are not enough for the severity of the dispute, the next step is to enforce military action. The UN peacekeeping efforts are initiated when the countries involved in a dispute or war are willing to resolve it through a peaceful political process. If this is true, why are the five permanent members of the Security Council (China, France, Russia, the United Kingdom, and the United States) having trouble enforcing complete sanctions on some ruthless dictators? Instead these unstable and volatile dictators are acquiring nuclear weapons from some developed countries in an attempt to defend themselves in case of military action by the UN.

There have been proposals to increase the number of permanent members of the Security Council from five to ten, but increasing the permanent member count will only make it more ineffective because that would mean more disagreeing hands could easily veto any resolution. Even with the current five members, China, Russia, and the United States mostly disagree on many issues. If the addition is absolutely required for proper representation, the list of additional members should include more stable developed countries and countries from the emerging markets.

The Economic and Social Council (ECOSOC) helps the General Assembly endorse economic and social development; membership from the Middle East and Africa are more suitable for ECPSOC membership rather than Security Council membership. ECOSOC sets policies for a number of funds under the UN like the Children's Fund and the Population Fund. None of them have yearly qualitative and quantitative realistic goals attached to them. It's not enough to provide responsibilities in all international socioeconomic development objectives but also tie qualitative and quantitative goals into them. If the employees of these funds are given goals and expectations that are tied to their pay scales, they will strive to meet these goals and expectations, making these organizations more effective. Making these funds more effective will also ease input of money from other charities into these funds and that will significantly reduce the duplication of efforts. ECOSOC works with a number of independent organizations called the specialized agencies, including the World Bank and IMF, to coordinate developmental activities around the world. While strengthening the responsibilities of ECOSOC in all socioeconomic development activities was a major step toward efficiency, it also gave corrupt developing and underdeveloped countries easy access to the money from the World Bank and IMF that is being exploited for personal gains.

Thorough background checks of these corrupt leaders should be done by independent bodies that are not in any way associated with the crooks, so that decisions can be made as to who gets access to these international lenders. If background checks of the achievement history of these corrupt leaders are not possible, then extensive investigation ought to be done as to how the money would be used by the leaders. Once they get approved, continuous monitoring of the project or projects should be done and any derail in project plans should be properly explained. The only way these corrupt leaders will learn any lesson is by tough rules that will deny them future loans if a project's funds are misused.

The secretary general's main function may be to help resolve international disputes and oversee peacekeeping initiatives, but he also needs to be a charming public figure of the UN, mustering support for their cause. The high stakes game of international socioeconomic problem solving cannot be played from behind the scenes and better-known public figures should give the secretary-generals more airtime to increase his public credibility. While the UN should use hard power tactics on dictatorial regimes, smart power tactics are required to unleash the power of UN on developing and underdeveloped countries and make its programs more effective. There is no point in wasting funds on programs that are not working, and sometimes even commonsense approaches to the problems in developing and underdeveloped countries just don't work. Most of the secretary-generals have been passive, but the secretary general should take decisive action to resolve international disputes and should not hesitate to punish the rascals who have repeatedly abused human rights.

A man like President Obama would make a very effective secretary general who would bring valuable changes to the unit, focusing on world peace and punishing those who don't. In fact President Obama should consider running for the position and taking his slogan Yes we can to the UN after he successfully finishes his two terms as the president.

Who cares if International Court of Justice (ICJ) is made up of ten or fifteen judges if it only represents a showcase justice system? The Security Council should be blamed for not bringing real international criminal cases in front of these judges, There's got be one member or nonmember state in the UN who is bold enough to bring the dictators to the ICJ and then hunt them down once they are convicted. What is the point of crying a river about human rights violations by these dictators if justice cannot be served to the innocent civilians of these countries? The Security Council members and non-members, along with the ICJ judges, should stop sitting on their bums and twiddling their thumbs in this serious matter. ICJ prosecutors need to take a more aggressive stance and bring as many controversial cases to the courtroom as possible, giving priority to issues that need immediate attention. In the case of the dictators and warlords who are running around in their countries scot-free with nobody to report to, it would be a unanimous decision between the Security Council and the ICJ regarding their heinous crimes against their own countrymen. If scoundrels like Slobodan Milosevic and many others in Africa can be tried for war crimes and genocides, why not take the many oppressive dictators and their regimes to trial in these international criminal courts? These below-average scums have harmed millions of people and their punishment should be either life in prison or death by injection.

Dismantling of the G77 would clear up two billion dollars of its yearly budget that could be used in various chapters of the UN for the economic reforms of the developing countries and for the upkeep of the UN peacekeeping forces. Peacekeeping forces have a dangerous and demanding job that needs quick reflexes and dynamic negotiation tactics to work with the raw, volatile emotions of people. It is only appropriate to distribute the G77 budget into maintaining the UN peacekeeping forces since most of the peacekeeping missions are in developing and underdeveloped countries. This will force the responsible governments to discourage people from resuming hostilities after a ceasefire. Even though we made a significant leap as a civilized world long time ago, there are still pockets of unrest around the world. People in these pockets have to eventually learn how to cope with their emotions to live a successful positive life like in the developed world. In Africa, there is so much hatred and recklessness between people of two different tribes from the same region; that combined with an utter lack of respect for any kind of law means thousands of peacekeepers have their hands full containing the emotions of these mostly uneducated and immature tribesmen. Sometimes there is only one peacekeeping Blue Helmet for every fifty or hundred refugees, but what better way to calm them down than to say their government is paying for all these Blue Helmets, and the more they fight, more it's going to cost their government. These refugees may have killed millions of tribesmen, women, and children, but it's the social responsibility of the peacekeepers to forgive their animal instincts and try to tame. The leaders who instigate these bloody battles should be tried in courts and killed or jailed for their actions.

Proceedings from the Perez-Guerrero Trust Fund for Economic and Technical Cooperation of Developing Countries (PGTF), which was established for the purpose of achieving national or collective self-reliance of developing countries, should be equally split among the various UN chapters. The fund was named after Manuel Perez-Guerrero who was a distinguished Venezuelan with a career in international civil service and high-level government office; he served as the secretary general of UNCTAD, which made outstanding contributions to the international community of developing nations. The fund and its name should be retained not only for the vast amounts of projects it has invested in, but also because, unlike the current Venezuelan dictator Chavez, Perez-Guerrero worked to uplift the people in his country.

Creating various chapters of the UN will enhance economic cooperation on trade among neighboring countries that will eventually lead to political cooperation among them. Not only will it enhance trade ties and global trade but also increase scientific research in developing and underdeveloped countries, with help of research ties from developed nations in their chapters.

Chapter 6
I Am a Billionaire So Let Me Help You

Four of the ten richest men in India are busy expanding their business empires and have very little or no time for charitable contributions. That's not the case in the developed world, and although a number of people in developed countries may make charitable donations for tax purposes, they're prompted to give because their donations help those in need. The mindset of people in developing countries is to mostly help themselves get ahead; they don't believe in making charitable contributions. Most people in developed countries also believe in secular humanism, which gives them a true concern for this life, a commitment to make life meaningful, a concern for fulfillment, growth, and creativity for themselves and others, and a conviction to build a better world for everybody. This ideology is starkly in contrast with the religious humanism that most people in developing countries follow. They seek profound religious experiences between God and themselves and don't necessarily believe in giving to aid the betterment of others. They believe in enriching their spiritual lives and are happy to earn enough to satisfy themselves and their family. People in developing countries don't believe in giving their hard-earned money away; this could be because most of these people were once in need of help or another reason could be that tax laws do not favor charitable giving. The fact that corruption is everywhere and local charities or the government might not spend the money appropriately could prevent charitable giving. These people are too ignorant to conduct research and find out which charities are legitimate and donate accordingly.

Charitable foundations/nonprofit organizations (NPO) engage in activities of public or private interest without any monetary profit. NPOs are active in various fields, including environment, animal protection, education, social issues, and healthcare. A lot of the rich in developed countries, including the top two richest billionaires in the world, are actively involved in a number of charitable foundations/NPOs. Billionaires, millionaires, and a lot of mainstream citizens of the developed world have a mindset of helping out fellow citizens, their country, and citizens in other countries in every way they can. A lot of these rich have built large successful companies, want to give something back to the community, and make a huge difference in the world in a positive way. It is alarming and concerning that the rich leaders of the business empires in India have no time for charity when there are millions of poor in their cities dying due to various diseases.

Due to the amount of population, even the small amount of charity work that some people do is not enough to help the poor and the ill. Of the five top 10 richest billionaires who are from the developing world, none have much interest in charitable work compared to that of the billionaires from the developed world. The developing world's pathetic uncharitable mindset was made evident when Mexico's billionaire businessman Carlos Slim poked fun at Bill Gates and Warren Buffett's philanthropy and claimed businessmen could do more good to the society by building good companies than donating money like Santa Claus. Although Slim set up a $450 million foundation for health research and care, it is negligible compared to his net worth and what his counterparts in the developed country are doing. Building companies may help some lucky people to come out of poverty by getting jobs in these companies, Slim must not have thought about other millions of unlucky ones who don't even have the basic necessities of shelter, healthcare and education let alone a decent job to feed them and their families. Slim built his empire by charging high prices for telephone lines in a country where more than 30 million people live on less than $2 per day. It is surprising to see that the rich from the developing countries believe that social programs are the duty of the government even though the government hardly has the budget to invest in these required-but-less-prioritized programs.

The other mindset of the rich in developed countries is that if family or friends have been inflicted with some deadly disease, they will jump in to donate or start a charity that will significantly fund the research to find a cure.

Charitable and humanitarian causes are given so much priority that educational institutions in the United States offer courses in international development studies; students taking these courses must perform volunteer work as part of the curriculum. I had a chance to talk to a number of American university students and learned that they all perform and enjoy volunteer work, which they did outside of their full-time job. This is unheard of in developing countries, where students are consumed by their family activities or entertainment activities. In 2007, over 60 million Americans students and professionals gave time to volunteer activities. In contrast, none or very few students from the Indian Institute of Technology and Indian Institute of Management, which are considered to be on par with the Ivy League, donate their time to volunteer activities. This holds true for professionals.

While there are a number of charitable foundations in India, not many people put time, effort, or money into these foundations. This means foundations do far less significant work than their counterparts in the developed world. Even the American movie industry is big on contributing to many charities, and celebrities take advantage of the media to promote these charities so more people donate to them. Bollywood should take note and make an example by generously donating to charities and take advantage of the huge media exposure in India to promote charities to the huge fan base of their celebrities. Charity telethons are a creative way for television media to bring charities to viewers' attention. Telethons are very popular and effective in raising money for charities in the United States but are unheard of in developing countries—the first ever was held in 2005 to help victims of the tsunami tragedy. With television viewers growing exponentially in India, charities should use TV to their advantage. Raising money after a disaster only slows the recovery process; the most cost effective way would be to hold annual telethons.

Experts believe that a continuous flow of aid from the developed world creates a poverty trap for citizens of the underdeveloped world. The poverty trap is self-inflicted by the citizens of the underdeveloped nations who are taking advantage of the aid and significantly stagnating their growth. The underdeveloped countries maintain chaos to continue receiving aid. The fact that China alone has invested over $100 billion in Africa since the year 2000 and it has not made a positive difference in its economic growth shows the state these underdeveloped countries.

Extreme poverty should be eradicated from the world population, especially in underdeveloped and low-income developing countries. Helping the citizens improve the vast majority of indices would automatically improve individual and national economic growth. The Point Four Program started by President Harry Truman to provide economic aid to poor and underdeveloped countries was an attempt to rebuild after World War II. That sort of aid program should not be used in the reconstruction of underdeveloped countries that are wrecked by their out-of-control civil wars. Those programs to unstable, underdeveloped countries should be stopped, as it has become a for-profit initiative between the companies involved and the corrupt leaders. Since stable, uncorrupt governments are hard to come by in underdeveloped countries, one alternative is for the aid agencies to completely circumvent the governments and work directly with the people, so that money does not land on corrupt government officials.

While the developed world is making sure the underdeveloped world is not neglected and keeps itself healthy, it should stop the habit of blindly providing financial aid to underdeveloped countries because it has become a lose-lose situation where the developed world is continually losing money to the underdeveloped countries that are in a rut with no way out. There are a number of countries that were underdeveloped and are currently categorized as developing after decades of incremental progress due to the hard work of its citizens and continuous change in their mindset. Underdeveloped countries should stop taking free rides from foreign financial aid that is creating lost generations due to nonexistent personal growth. Aid by itself is not bad, but it is bad when the governments of underdeveloped countries take advantage of it for their own personal gains.

The secondary motive of aid to underdeveloped countries is to show them the power of money and the positive influence they could be to the people all over the world by transforming their mindset to bring changes to their lives. It is utterly ridiculous for people to think that free financial aid to underdeveloped African countries led to corruption because corruption in underdeveloped and developing countries is a way of life and a state of mind. Aid has only increased the scale of corruption. If the people in these underdeveloped countries had the will to make changes in their lives for the better, they could have done it even in the midst of rampant corruption.

Although the UN Millennium Project and Millennium Development Goals are striving to significantly reduce world poverty by 2015, it seems unlikely that they will be successful. While I totally agree with the expert creators of the UN Millennium Development Goals on the points of utilizing family planning techniques to alleviate poverty and curb the spread of AIDS in underdeveloped countries, I totally disagree with the experts who push maintaining or increasing foreign aid. Drastic measures are needed to change the mindset of the underdeveloped, and transforming foreign aid to loan programs that force governments to be responsible is essential. Part of the aid problem is the origin of the aid supplies, and if the experts insist on maintaining foreign aid, an easier and alternative way to achieve UN Millennium Development Goals would be to encourage satisfying local demands with local supplies who should be given subsidies to improve their yields. Not only would those in need receive aid, but also using local businesses would boost the country's economic growth after stable and effective governments are formed.

Economist and international public affairs expert Jeffrey Sachs recommends that the aid organizations should conduct themselves as venture capitalists and fund businesses in underdeveloped nations that are run by locals. This would give the citizens a sense of responsibility. What Mr. Sachs neglects to see is that for venture capitalism to work in these underdeveloped nations, people must first change their mindsets by forming stable governments. Start-up funding in the middle of political unrest won't work and that is exactly why no significant foreign investments are made in these countries. A change in mindset could do wonders in these underdeveloped countries, but a lack of motivation, combined with continuous foreign aid, has put them in a financial rut. It is not only a poverty trap or financial rut for underdeveloped countries but also a financial burden for the developed world.

While the underdeveloped countries struggle to survive despite the massive aid provided to them, a number of charities from the developed world are continuously trying to make the lives of the people in these poor underdeveloped countries better. The only inefficiency is that some charities are working to resolve the same issues. It would be best if the charities working on the same issue collaborated so they don't duplicate work. For this to happen, charitable foundations should make themselves more transparent both to their benefactors and to other charities. Transparency aids efficiency and also improves public confidence because people are often skeptical about how their donation would be used.

Not all billionaires in the developed world donate to charities, but some like Bill Gates and Warren Buffett are making a huge impact with their charitable giving. As soon as Gates was number one on Forbes list of the World's Richest People, public opinion built up toward his charitable expectations, and he immediately started studying the works of charitable greats Andrew Carnegie and John D. Rockefeller. In 2000 he founded the Bill and Melinda Gates Foundation and drew his long time bridge partner Buffett into his philanthropic efforts. Satisfied with the Gates Foundation's charity work, Buffett pledged to give away 10 million class B shares of his investment company (worth over $30 billion) over a number of years provided Gates was involved in the charity's operations. All these huge donations are big enough to make significant life changes to a number of communities around the world. The Gates Foundation has grown from $2 billion to $38 billion while working on enhancing health care, reducing poverty in developing and underdeveloped countries, and expanding educational opportunities and access to American information technology.

Indian born billionaire and steel tycoon Laxmi Mittal who lives in the United Kingdom made annual $10 million charitable contributions but spent $180 million on a mansion and about $80 million on his daughter's wedding. Mittal who is on the Forbes top-ten billionaires list, definitely doesn't see the need to be quite as socially responsible as his U.S. counterparts, and the difference in numbers is quite startling. The American dream is as free as the country, with the dream ultimately blossoming into social responsibility carried on by others; the Indian dream is as selfish as its government. Some of these billionaires have an emotional attachment to and pride in their enormous possessions. They don't understand why anyone would want to just give money away. But they have to know that they are not going to take all that accumulated wealth with them to the grave, so they should put it to good use for their family and others.

Each person has the right to spend money as he or she wants, but the rich have to realize that they also have social responsibilities. They should contribute to the significant improvement of mankind not just by creating jobs but also through charitable donations. Also it is not enough for the rich in the developing world to work on reducing poverty; they must work collaboratively to instill foundations that work on a larger scale for the enhancement of the human development index. Just as in case of space research and development, Indian charitable contributors only believe in solving the immediate practical problems that are affecting the people and don't believe in solving higher problems that will enhance the condition of the human race as a whole. Apart from the size of the charitable contributions, the difference between the contributors in the developed and the developing worlds is the far-sighted vision versus the near-sighted vision in terms of solving lingering problems affecting their fellow citizens. Once they make these significant contributions, the developing world will be almost on par with the developed world as far as human development index is concerned. Although not every rich person in the developing world donates a significant portion of his or her fortune for charitable causes, there are a incredible number of passionate geeks who only believe in giving back to the society.

The charitable ones in the developed world especially in the US are a dynamic bunch that swam in the vast ocean of social responsibilities despite their physical or mental handicaps. Take in the case of billionaire entrepreneur and marvelous aviator Howard Hughes who in spite of constant bizarre episodes of erratic behaviors that could be categorized into borderline mental illness still had the presence of mind to start a charitable organization called The Howard Hughes Medical Institute (HHMI) to understand the genesis of life. HHMI is now the second best endowed medical research foundation in the world with donation money worth over $18 billion and annual investments in biomedical research of about $700 million. Howard was a certified passionate geek and a believer who at the young age of nineteen signed a will to create a medical research lab after his father's death. Howard founded the institute twenty-five years later in 1953 after transferring all his company stocks in Hughes Aircraft to HHMI making it the owner of a for-profit company, which turned a lot of heads in the Internal Revenue Service department. It remained a modest institute for couple of decades mainly due to Howard's eccentric obsession and severe addiction to pain medications but after Howard's death in 1976, the Institute refocused its research mission on genetics, immunology and molecular biology. Selling Hughes Aircraft stocks to GE helped the Institute to grow dramatically and eventually to focus its research in neurobiology understanding information processing by neuronal circuits and developing computational methods for image analysis. Even certified geeks and more stable businessmen in a developing country like India including the Tatas and Narayana Murthy of the famed software service company Infosys have not made significant contributions in the national or international level but rather have made small contributions in the field of education locally. The difference is quite evident not only because of nonexistence of charitable foundations from the wealthy but also due to the passive nature of small amount of charities with no promotional activities. The mindset of caring and giving to the underprivileged and the needy in the United States has existed since the seventeenth century. At the time, efforts were focused at the neighborhood level, but there were a number of proposals by big-hearted and visionary individuals to resolve social issues such as taking care of the poor. As time passed, the small and unorganized charitable gifts from the wealthy and the middle-class grew into an influential and organized movement with the goal of improving the conditions of the poor. Although critics claim the visionaries during that time didn't do enough, putting the idea forth and laying a solid foundation for social services was the most valuable achievement and stepping-stone for future generations. These charitable visionaries should be commended for their commitment to finding resolutions for the complex social issues of their day. In contrast, the wealthy and those in power in developing countries in the twenty-first century have the resources to help resolve social issues by investing in charitable foundations, but disappointingly they don't have the mindset to make charitable giving a habit.

John D. Rockefeller took the models and paths created by the early visionaries of charitable giving one step further and gave away ten percent of his earnings, starting with his first paycheck. All in all he gave away over $500 million to noble causes during his lifetime and his legacy continues through his charitable foundation. Rockefeller was influenced by Andrew Carnegie, who gave away most of his money. There has been continuous growth of charitable foundations in the United States generation after generation, and all credit should be given to the early visionaries who sowed the seeds of charitable giving. After Carnegie and Rockefeller, the next generation of philanthropists included the Ford family, which established the Ford Foundation in 1936. In 2007 the foundation's assets totaled over $13 billion.

When comparing the charitable achievements of the Ford family to that of the Tata family, which now owns the Jaguar and Land Rover auto companies, the Tata family is put to shame. Ford Foundation annual grant for 2007 was $530 million for projects that helped human rights, the environment, community and economic development, media, education, arts, and culture. Recognizing the lack of caring and giving attitude in the aftermath of British rule in India, the Ford Foundation even established its first international field office in New Delhi in 1952. Unfortunately none of the wealthy Indian businessmen took the hint and developed homegrown charitable organizations. While the Tata family has made mentionable contributions in the field of medicine, education, arts, and culture, they haven't made any dent in the field of charitable contributions in India due to the size of population in poverty. It would be incredible for the Tata Foundation to tie with U.S. and European foundations, but if it did, it would put India on the world charitable foundation map and make significant progress toward increasing its human development index. To their credit, the Tata Foundation did help launch the small-loan offering Grameen Bank in Bangladesh that has been a huge hit in that country.

Foundations in developing countries aren't working to reduce poverty in their own country because they believe that is the responsibility of the government. There is definitely a need for charitable leadership in developing countries, so the wealthy have a clear direction for social responsibility. It is this leadership and direction laid by early visionaries in the developed world, especially in the United States that has created a wealth of charitable foundations.

William Hewlett started the William and Flora Hewlett Foundation in 1967 and the Foundation has net assets of over $8 billion working on a number of education programs with elite institutions like MIT and Stanford. Hewlett Foundation not only focused its goals on changing and improving instructions in public schools and community colleges but also on improving student achievement and graduation rates. To make the most out of the available resources, foundations in developing countries should focus both on qualitative and quantitative improvements in a number of areas that desperately need help. The Hewlett Foundation is also involved in a number of environmental issues all over the world and that's another area where foundations in developing countries need to get involved in due to increased growth and continuous environmental neglect. While these private foundations are doing a huge amount of difference in communities all over the world, the work by public non-profit organizations is even bigger due to a large amount of volunteers. Even in the case of public nonprofit organizations, the developing world is far behind the developed world not only in the number of volunteers but also the amount of money raised. While Amnesty International (AI) in the United Kingdom, with its simple mission to protect human rights, boasts over two million members, ASHA in India is yet to see the large-scale success of which its founders once dreamed. For AI, it all started one fine day in

1960, when Peter Benenson read about two Portuguese students who were sentenced to seven years of imprisonment for raising their glasses as a toast to freedom. Benenson, with help from his friends, published a newspaper article condemning the act. The article, which was reprinted by several international newspapers, described human rights violations by governments marking the launch of Appeal for Amnesty for the two Portuguese students. What started as an appeal to release the students became a permanent international movement to protect people who expressed their views nonviolently. People in developing countries should be as spontaneous in their charitable instincts and go with their gut feelings when they feel the need for change or assistance. Passivity will not change the lives of millions of underprivileged people. These kinds of organizations don't become a hit with the volunteers overnight; it takes tremendous leadership effort and persistent drive for them to succeed.

Sometimes these leaders need to witness a large-scale human tragedy to be moved to action. That's what happened to Swiss businessman Henry Dunant in 1859, when he met Napoleon III in the small town of Solferino. Instead of discussing business with Napoleon III, he witnessed the Battle of Solferino in the Austro-Sardinian War. About forty thousand people either died or were wounded in a single day, and the suffering of the wounded and the lack of basic medical attendance shocked Dunant. He canceled his meeting with Napoleon III in favor of helping the wounded soldiers with their treatment, and he ushered the local people to assist the wounded soldiers. He later wrote a book about his experience in Solferino and called for the formation of voluntary relief organizations to nurse wounded soldiers in times of war. He sent copies of his book to political and military figures in Europe and in 1863 formed a commission with five of his friends to investigate the possibility of forming a relief organization. Later that year the commission organized a conference to discuss improving medical services during war and thus Red Cross was born. Today the International Red Cross boasts about 97 million volunteers worldwide and strives to protect human life and health, protect human rights, and alleviate human suffering without discrimination.

There are hardly any businessmen in developing countries that would cancel a business meeting to attend to the sufferings of the wounded in any tragedy, and even if they did, it would not result in the birth of a nonprofit organization as massive and effective as the Red Cross. Although relief efforts in India had been slow and chaotic but satisfying to some extent in the aftermath of the tsunami tragedy, no Indian charity organization has stepped up to be the next big charity. The Indian chapter of Red Cross is a good organization during disaster relief but there has to be a local nonprofit organization big enough to help at least one quarter of the poor with everyday issues during regular times. Hoping that day will come during my lifetime, I am praying to the Indian charitable gods to make it happen as soon as possible.

There are a number of other billionaires in the developed world who have made significant donations for a number of causes. Michael Bloomberg, who is the mayor of New York City and owner of Bloomberg LP, has gifted over $600 million to a number of health causes in the US and the rest of the world. Tobacco industry in the United States has undergone a massive overhaul with citizens and the government suing tobacco companies resulting in tobacco companies agreeing to pay states to cover the medical bills of patients with smoking-related illnesses. Many states have banned smoking in certain public areas like bars and restaurants so as to not affect passive smoking. Tobacco industry in developing countries like India is unregulated and ban of smoking in public places is unheard of. Realizing the need for some kind of tobacco regulations in many developing countries, Bloomberg together with Gates made a $500 million donation to help governments in developing countries with tobacco control. With issues like tobacco control especially in developing countries, these billionaires should make sure that they don't give the money directly to the corrupt and inefficient governments of these developing countries. Instead, these donations should go to non-profit organizations in those countries fighting against tobacco control so that the money goes to the actual cause while giving it to the corrupt governments would be a total waste. Also there should be an independent world research organization to overlook all charity and non-profit research economic distribution so the money is allocated as required and not spent disproportionately. Similar to Peterson Foundation's efforts to spread the need about fiscal responsibility, there should be an international charitable fiscal responsibility organization that would efficiently map out the world charitable supply and demand requirements so as to link the resources accordingly. When Peter G. Peterson became a billionaire as co-founder of Blackstone Group, instead of giving money away to charities, he decided to start a foundation that addressed federal budget deficit issues, healthcare issues, tax policies and the like. Developing countries not only need foundations like Peterson's but also more significant charities from billionaires of these countries to fight for the causes that would do the right thing. Most rags-to-riches stories in developed countries have a magnificent ending of significant social responsibility, whereas in developing countries they end in mundane family responsibilities and an excuse for social irresponsibility. Indian billionaire Azim Premji may be known for his modesty and frugality in his everyday life—driving a Toyota Corolla and flying economy class—but he extends his frugality to his foundation whose only achievement to date is releasing a number of educational CDs for Indian schoolchildren. That's a paltry philanthropic accomplishment by Premji when you compare it to an American billionaire like George Soros who has given away over $6 billion in three decades of philanthropy. While Carl Icahn is known for his contributions to homeless shelters and educational institutions, Pallonji Mistry and Sunil Mittal are unheard of in Indian philanthropic circles. Why is there so much difference between these billionaires in their philanthropic efforts? Why is there so much attachment to money by billionaires in developing countries? Since no Indian politicians have the credibility to preach to the business community about philanthropy, the president should regularly reach out to the business community about the need for them to increase their social responsibility. To start with, the millionaires and the billionaires of India should give away at least ten percent of their income to charities that fund life-altering work that improves the human development index.

Businesses in developing countries should be ashamed of their lack of philanthropic efforts because in the United States even the infamous Playboy Enterprises, with which every teenage boy all around the world is familiar, has given away over $10 million for religious, scientific, and educational causes over forty years. This kind of philanthropy by businesses in developing countries is unheard of and demonstrates that social responsibility is an acquired mindset. Businesses and businessmen in developing countries need a philanthropic push from credible leaders to convince them of the need for social responsibility. If Playboy can do it, so can all the conglomerates, millionaires, and billionaires in developing countries. The governments in developing countries can encourage charitable donations by increasing the tax benefits to donors. The governments in these countries can't preach the value of philanthropy because of its lack of philanthropic leanings; the only other way to encourage people is by providing monetary benefits.

The problem is that the millionaires and billionaires in developing countries are not passionate about bringing change to their society, but in developed countries, you can't take the charities out of the millionaires and billionaires. One multimillionaire or billionaire should take the initiative to make significant charitable contributions while employing huge positive media coverage and the rest of them will follow. Socially responsible millionaires and billionaires in developed countries are usually married and have huge families, and yet they don't shy away from giving for greater causes.

It's not only the playboys, but also athletes who are involved in charitable contributions and after retirement give full-time attention, helping disadvantaged youths reach their full athletic potential. Tennis star Andre Agassi started his charitable foundation while he was still a professional athlete and has raised over $60 million to help at-risk children. No professional cricket players in India, active or retired, are actively involved in any charitable foundations. Agassi just didn't stop with his foundation but went a step further to create a charity called Athletes for Hope, along with a number of other leading athletes in the country to help other athletes get involved in charitable causes. Seven times Tour de France winner and cancer survivor Lance Armstrong has raised over $250 million for cancer research and support. Sports celebrities in developing countries seem to fall out of the spotlight after their career and hardly ever get involved in charities or lend their celebrity status to further socially responsible causes. If the achievements of Agassi and Armstrong seem huge, sports personalities in developing countries should take a lesson from professional skateboarder Tony Hawk about simple achievements. His foundation has taken up the simple mission of helping promote and finance public skate parks in a number of low-income neighborhoods in the United States. The beauty of this mission is their ulterior motives of helping kids keep themselves out of trouble (Hawk got himself in trouble before starting to skateboard). Why can't sports personalities in developing countries make simple efforts to help kids stay out of trouble? It's all smooth sailing once they get past the bureaucracies and corrupt practices, but informal social networking in skate parks or cricket grounds helps kids think outside the box and stay out of trouble.

The social irresponsibility of sports figures in India was so evident to sports figures from other countries that they decided to fill the void by creating foundations to help Indian kids. While Indian cricketer Sachin Tendulkar has started a little bit of educational help to kids, it is Australian cricketer Steve Waugh who has taken the bold step to set up an educational trust fund in the city of Calcutta that helps a number of underprivileged kids. It is so amazing to see Waugh become an inspiration to a number of these kids in India, but it feels a bit nauseating to see the Indian sports figures fade into oblivion after their stretch in the sports arena. These personalities in developing countries have the mindset that their job for the country is done by playing on the national team, and they need time for themselves and their families once they are retired. These personalities are public figures and should develop a mindset to continuously dedicate themselves to public causes that will enrich the lives of the deprived to build a better society. Just as the American dream extends beyond the free market system and into social responsibility for good causes, the dreams of the rich and famous in developing countries should balance between selfish and selfless causes.

Chapter 7

How Are the Others Doing?

A friend who had only been to Canada and the United States went on a trip to Mexico when she was twenty-years-old and was aghast at the way most people lived in small mud houses with poor sanitary conditions. I was initially perplexed at her agony but later realized that the homeless population in various cities in the developed world just evaporates amid the vast skyscrapers.

When you go to Australia, your subconscious mind will ignore any homeless people while you are busy watching the beauty of the kangaroo or the Sydney Opera House or the obsessive national pastime cricket. It's not just the subconscious but also the conscious mind of the government that spends over a billion dollars yearly to keep the homeless safe and secure in shelters. Maintaining a small resident population of a little over twenty million has kept their homeless population to less than 1 percent, which is in line with homelessness in other developed countries. They are even generous and socially responsible about the international communities providing over two billion dollars worth of aid and assistance.

Quite in contrast, the Indian government's paper-only programs for homelessness have put its number to an astronomical eighty million—close to 10 percent of the population. While the developed world tries to extend as much care as possible to their homeless citizens with various assistance programs, authorities in large cities in developing countries like India send beggars and homeless to jail for up to three years instead of offering any assistance to improve their lives. The homeless in India are perceived to be mentally ill and considered a burden since some of them use illegal electricity connections and most of them relieve themselves and bathe in public places. While the Indian government sponsors programs to provide night shelters and affordable housing, most of these programs are either not enough to help the significant population or don't see the light of day because of rampant corruption.

While Japan's hard work and determination has created an economic powerhouse, it also has given rise to increasing homelessness. Don't be distraught because this is not a depressing story, but a story of efficiency at its best that you will only see in a developed world. The highly literate Japanese population is innovative even when it comes to homelessness, and the urban homeless pay to use the cyber cafes to sleep, shower, and eat while the not-so-urban homeless grow their own vegetables in donated lands to feed themselves and collect wood to keep themselves warm at night. Only in a tight-knit and generous developed world can one see this kind of efficiency even when it comes to the distraught that sets them apart from the developing and the underdeveloped world. In a developing country, not only would one not see a homeless person take advantage of the bathroom facilities in an internet cafe or grow their own vegetable garden, they would be shut down immediately for trespassing by authorities.

The nonprofit organizations in developing and underdeveloped nations should increase their contributions to the needs of the homeless since the governments are incapable of serving the poor. Don't cancel your vacation to a developing country or an underdeveloped country because of these socio-economic issues because the natural and cultural beauty still exists in these countries.

The exceptional performance from developed countries comes with a reward and Australia was ranked third for its human development index (HDI), sixth in quality-of-life index, and GDP per capita growth higher than the United States and Canada. The Indian government deregulated its financial system less than ten years after the Australian government, but its HDI and quality-of-life index is significantly lower than Australia's. This consistently points to the fact that human development and quality-of-life indices are as important to a country's growth as its economy.

While Hitler's Germany can only be found in history books, there are still some radical leftist organizations that have been involved in violent hate crimes and adding insult to this injury is the economic, social, and cultural differences that continue between West and East Germans, even after almost two decades of reunification. While the country has one of the lowest birth rates in the world and a high aging population, it also has a considerable immigrant population despite the language barrier in a country where English is not spoken, written, or seen on displays or signs. The developed world should understand that in spite of the dangers of crazy terrorists infiltrating their countries, immigration is so important for the country's economic gain and also for changing the mindsets of immigrants, especially the ones from developing and underdeveloped countries. These immigrants from undernourished countries will learn the system in developed countries and one day return to their homelands to help teach the system they learned as immigrants to their friends, neighbors, relatives and fellow countrymen.

The developed world should increase the number of immigrants from the developing world allowed into their countries either to further their studies or get better jobs. The developed world should think of this as an indirect help to all the developing countries since the immigrant population sends money back to their home countries that will help the economic growth of that country. Critics may claim that this would increase the risk of letting dangerous elements into the country but with careful consideration of each applicant, including an extensive background check, this would be a positive situation for the developed world, developing world, and the people involved. This may also prompt an increased backlash from the native population of the developed world and hate crimes against immigrants, but the citizens should be informed that the influx of immigrants is always temporary.

Germany is the third largest economy in the world in terms of nominal GDP and is the largest economy in Europe. It is amazing to see how it recovered to prewar levels and continuously grew to present-day levels. The efficiency, quality, and productivity displayed by Germans is shown in the agriculture sector, which accounts for less than 1 percent of GDP but covers 90 percent of domestic needs. What's more amazing is that the tiny island nation of Japan, ravaged after World War II, has become the second largest economy in the world. It has not only built a strong government and economy but also a human development index that is no match to its Asian counterparts and industries that are renowned for exceptional quality and reliability.

Japan's obsession with the finer things in life put them in an awkward position with the international community, especially environmentalists because of the country's ravenous appetite for shark fins, whales, and dolphins. The Japanese fishing industry recklessly slaughtered these wonderful creatures to the point of being put on the endangered list. Sharks in the shallow waters around Japan are caught in significant numbers, but what shocked the international community was that after their fins were cut off these sharks were thrown back into the ocean to die. After repeated pleas from various environmental groups, the government signed international agreements and regulations to limit the killing, but the lure and smell of these delicacies could not keep the fishermen away for long. Calling these endangered creatures "cockroaches of the sea," one of Japan's fishing industry lobbyists who stood to lose a huge amount of profit referred to the regulations as Western cultural imperialism. It is sad to see that the Asian governments believe these much needed regulations as cultural imperialism while they completely fail to notice the fishing industry's reckless attitude towards sharks. It is absolutely flabbergasting to see this kind of irresponsible treatment of endangered animals from citizens of a developed country. It is ironic that they take care of their homeless beings on land but are very cruel to the helpless fish in the vast ocean.

It's not just the Japanese who are at fault, but fishing industries everywhere that are feeding into the shark-eating frenzy of rich Asians who would comfortably pay one hundred dollars to savor the shark-fin dish. In spite of the limitations on the amount of sharks killed for fins, the trade flourishes because of demand; fishermen will only heed the limits when demand is curtailed either by the restaurants or the public. The restaurants can do their part by limiting their daily demand of sharks while increasing their offerings of other dishes to the public and giving special discounts on other dishes. The governments should give special shark fin ratings and tax subsidies to restaurants that limit the shark fin dish consumption by their customers. Until the Japanese start treating their sharks the same or even better than their homeless population, the international tree-hugging environmentalists should descend on this nation to make them stop this madness. Where are the tree-hugging environmentalists when you really need them? Somebody please wake them up from their trees so they can go save some sharks.

The automobile, consumer electronics, and computer manufacturers maybe successfully competing with other global brands in this field but what's more mesmerizing is their extra gentleness in the food industry. The Japanese food and food processing industries are worth close to one trillion dollars. Japanese Kobe beef is known for its extra tenderness, which is attributed to the special attention the cattle receive daily, including alcohol, soothing music for their ears and massages. If you think this is funny, wait till you find out about all the wild and outrageous Japanese game shows that have been catching on around the world. Watching these shows will definitely leave you cracking up on the floor. What's not funny and won't make you crack up is the fact that Japanese individuals and corporations are lagging way behind the rest of the developed world in their philanthropic efforts. They should cut down on their consumption of shark-fin soup and Kobe beef, and donate the savings to charitable causes.

Environmental damage and charitable donations are serious matters, but issues regarding an individual's sexual preferences should only be a topic of light discussion over coffee. Many countries in Europe have the most liberal laws when it comes to same-sex partnerships, and the United Kingdom is no different. It allows same-sex couples to register as civil partners and extends almost all the rights of marriage to registered partners. While many other European countries have allowed same-sex couples to be civil partners, many American states are still struggling with coming to a decision, and a lot of developing countries are not even close to accepting any kind of same-sex relationships. It is surprising to see that majority of European immigrants in the United States have become extremely conservative after crossing the Atlantic.

The developed and the developing worlds are at different stages of accepting same-sex relationships into the mainstream progressive and the conservative worlds. While the developed world went through the same-sex relationship evolution and the phase of homophobia a long time ago, the developing minds in India that are religiously conservative are going through the homophobic phase in this first decade of the twenty-first century. During this phase in the United States, there were a number of same-sex hate crimes, including some deaths, but most of the crimes against same-sex partners in India have involved verbal and physical abuse by family members or sexual abuse by strangers. Although homosexuality is mentioned in various ancient Indian sagas and love guides, the religious conservatives of the twenty-first century are angry because they believe same-sex relationships are an attack on deep traditions. They consider same-sex partnership issue in the country as a prey of a clandestine queer invasion from the developed world. It has been hard on the mindset of the religious conservative in India as the family values has been traditionally limited to no dating and arranged marriages between a man and a woman. When a developing society has social issues that are difficult to fathom by the moderate but religious conservative mind, they usually blame it on somebody else, so the society still appears perfect with no stains. In extremely religious societies like Iran and Iraq, organized campaigns have been set up to kill homosexuals who they believe are a blemish to their society. It is so disturbing to see that the religious extremists who have been taught since childhood that a relationship is only between a man and a woman and can only happen after marriage cannot justify a homosexual relationship but can easily justify all their heinous killings.

If two human beings, whether two males or two females or a male and female, are attracted to each other and want to have a relationship, then the society should accept this without any animosity or bias. The society should also let these couples take their relationship to the next level and confirm their love in marriage, and not harp on age-old traditional ways of life. The gay and lesbian community, along with the gay and lesbian rights group in India, should keep their fight alive, and as it happened in the developed world, the conservative government and the mainstream society will accept these communities. This may take a little longer in the developing world due to its deep-rooted traditions that are hard to change.

The liberal views of European countries are not only limited to sex and nudity, but also to environmental protection—specifically wetland preservation. Most of Europe and Asian countries have no wetland regulations and have very few nonprofit organizations that take care of preserving existing wetlands in their countries. The United States, by comparison, has very strict regulations to maintain its wetlands and anybody who disrupts the ecological balance of the wetlands is required by law to either create their own wetlands or buy credits from existing wetlands as compensation. European and Asian countries need to step up their environmental regulations and enforcement activities, including preserving and expanding wetlands that are so crucial to not only preserve wildlife but also to reduce soil erosion, cleaning pollution, and storing carbon dioxide. There is plenty of space on this earth for countries to grow their industries to accommodate their economic growth, but this should not come at the expense of destroying our environment. We must consider future generations and take steps to ensure they don't live in environmental distress because of this generation's decisions.

As seen in previous chapters, the socioeconomic landscape changes dramatically in developing countries when compared with the developed ones and sometimes, similar issues are handled differently because of different mindsets. As the saying goes, old habits die hard, and some developing mindsets don't change even if they have a developed nation as an example nearby.

Like any developing country, Armenia is trying to address its environmental problems, with taxes for air and water pollution, and solid waste disposal. Armenians living abroad support the economy by their investment and that is one of the main reasons the country is still underdeveloped in terms of waste management and recycling. Expatriates living in developed economies should not only support the economy back home but also provide ideas to profitably save the environment. People in these countries should stop waiting for government legislation about waste disposal and recycling, and take action to save the environment and make them profitable. The problem of waste disposal is enormous, and even a small country as Armenia has over fifty landfills, without waste sorting, reusing, or recycling. Can you imagine the amount of pollution these landfills create everyday?

In the United States, not only do household recycle but the subject has been introduced into the country's primary and secondary educational system. Governments and nonprofit organizations in developing and underdeveloped countries should work on incorporating these trivial but life-changing subjects into their educational systems because the first person who is going to make this simple change in lifestyle would be the kids. In the United States, a city with a population of a little over seven hundred thousand was easily making more than a million dollars in revenue from its recycling program, and one can imagine the revenue the cities in countries like India and China could bring from its recycling programs with their populations. This will also give millions of poor rag pickers (as they are called in India) who move around cities picking recyclable materials from trashcans a legitimate job. It gives employment to the poor, cleans cities, and saves the environment and also gives some credibility to the governments for making a simple contribution to turn the lives of many poor lives. Again the governments in these countries should hand over the recycling, composting, and incinerating process to the private sector for effective handling of business.

The government of India finally woke up in 2005 regarding policies on e-waste recycling and encouraging the business community to set up recycling plants. But the government quickly dozed off while e-waste kept growing at an alarming rate. E-waste in India and most developing and underdeveloped countries should be one of the most important social issues agenda on the table for the government and the media to debate and devise strategies for successfully bringing it under control.

Sometimes corporations in developed countries that operate in developing countries seem to take advantage of a slack government and law enforcement. These corporations that stick to stringent environmental laws in the developed world should uphold the same routine in the developing world. Most people in those developing or underdeveloped countries may be uneducated and wouldn't understand the meaning of environmental laws, but it only takes one educated person among them to take these multinational companies to court. This happened in Ecuador when Texaco was polluting the Amazon River and rainforest. The lesson here is that regardless of where a company operates, the company should adhere to common company practice.

The countries that willingly act as toxic dumping grounds are putting their citizens in danger and should be held responsible as willing participants in the poisoning of its citizens for personal gain. Who is going to clean all this toxic mess up? Are these governments a bunch of stupid, ignorant, socially irresponsible punks that are not able to think within reason, let alone outside the box? What are they thinking? God is certainly not going to feel pity and clean it up with a wave of his magical wand.

Both the United States and British India are credited with starting the conservation movement and both have come a long way compared to India, even after the progressive era that urged the establishment of state and national parks and forests, wildlife refuges, and national monuments. The United States stuck to the conservation movement throughout the centuries, but India neglected it as soon as the British left the country to concentrate on a number of other issues plaguing the country. As always, the Indian government is ineffective and hence nonprofit organizations with environmental concerns should work with individual environmentalists to take matters into their own hands. As a team the nonprofit organizations and the environmentalists should effectively work with the government and other concerned entities to come up with a valuable resolution that will maintain the environmental balance.

Two emerging economies in two different parts of the world—Brazil and India—have some common social issues like education, gender gap, corruption, and the environment, but the one that's going to come out ahead depends on which government will lay out laws and regulations to resolve these issues successfully. It looks like Brazil is already ahead since it is trying to kill two birds with one stone—closing gender gap and eliminating corruption—by promulgating a regulation that will require that each political party consist of at least 30 percent of either gender. Were they thinking gorgeous women in Brazil are easier to corrupt by including them in political parties? The economic visions and actions of emerging-markets governments look retarded when compared to developed countries' economic growth.

The gender gap in developed and emerging economies is mild compared to the gap in underdeveloped economies. The combined leadership of Taliban and Al-Qaeda abused human rights rules and mistreated women, using and abusing them as they wished. The regime forced women to wear the burqa in public, banned them from school and work after the age of eight, and executed them if they were caught in violation of the laws. Only narcissistic pigs would do anything like that to put women down. Male doctors couldn't treat women unless accompanied by a male family member, women faced flogging in the public, and everyone faced public execution for violations of Sharia law. While an average of one in five women is abused physically or sexually in developed countries, it is also a global phenomenon that differs in numbers and extent of the abuse depending on how actively the government enforces its domestic violence laws and a number of other personal factors. Due to lack of government enforcement and a number of other social and economic factors, about 70 percent of married women are abused in a developing country like India. Abuse and victimization of women is much more prevalent in underdeveloped countries like Afghanistan. The law there is based on ancient ideology and the radical interpretations of Islam favored by fundamentalist organizations, but it has been changed to fit the twisted psyche of these Neanderthal and negative mindsets. The most extreme case of the alpha male character displayed by the Al-Qaeda and Taliban members is their refusal to include or acknowledge women in their organization; they believe a woman's role to be limited to taking care of the home and children. Women are treated as objects, not of display but of despair. Women have no place to express their frustrations and must silently endure their sufferings.

They want the women in their country to be illiterate and ignorant, so that they never demand the true love and respect they deserve from their men.

No person should be elected or selected solely because of their race, gender, or caste; instead, leaders should be chosen based on their merit, giving equal opportunity to everyone, and other signs of a progressive democratic government. On the contrary, more and more women in the developed world are out-earning their men or becoming the only source of income for the family, while the men are comfortable doing household chores and being stay-at-home dads. As these dynamic men get adjusted to their new roles in the family, they still feel comfortable and confident as the head of household and protector of their women.

Chapter 8
I Am Stupid and Live in a Fantasyland

George Bernard Shaw once said that all progress depends on the unreasonable man since he persists in trying to adapt the world to himself versus the reasonable man who adapts himself to the world. True in the case of developed and developing minds. Certainly not true in the case of the stupid terrorists whose unreasonable characteristics only destroy the world. The radical thinkers want to eliminate the jahili society (meaning ignorant or un-Islamic), as well as their concepts and traditions. I believe in the concept of live and let live. If one wants to lead a certain lifestyle, he is free to do so. But no one can tell other societies how to lead their lives. If one wants to lead a caveman's life, go right ahead. But don't force or expect everybody else to join you. It is very disturbing that the students of these radical thinkers have learned a different ideology from their preachers and are then confused by mainstream society. It is the clash of two different ways of life—one backward and bound by sentimental and radical religious beliefs and the other modern and realistic but sometimes bound by moderate religious beliefs.

The extremist ideology of promoting violence has nothing to do with childhood abuse and trauma as some experts claim but is due to the teaching of hatred to kids about religions and the notion of perceived injustice. These radical religious beliefs stem from years of preaching hatred to their kids in schools and results in the destruction of the lives of these kids who otherwise would have grown up to be wonderful loving human beings. Imagine a kid being tied to a chair all his life without ever walking; when he or she is let go from the chair, one can't expect him or her to walk immediately. At the end of the day it is what one believes in that matters and these radical-thinking terrorists have been fed hate-filled ideas for a number of years.

Although I am not sure if God exists, I do believe that there is some superpower in nature independent of religions that keeps the earth together and keeps this wonderful life cycle going. The radical-thinking terrorists are frustrated and are seeking attention, but if they want the government authorities to listen to them, they need to stop annoying people with their belief in hatred. Instead, they should start believing in love for all human beings. I may not believe in religion, but everybody has their right to believe in God and religion, as long as it does not lead to violence. If the radical thinkers were to put themselves in the shoes of a moderate thinker, they would see the world as a much happier place and lead their lives in a much happier way. Radical thinkers who create terror by bombing and killing innocent people need to understand that they are only belittling themselves in the minds of moderate thinkers and are throwing their lives away by conducting these stupid acts. Religions were started to promote group togetherness in a way that gave people solace and comfort.

Radical militants who use violent methods only show that they are weak. They cannot keep up with the modern world and are showing their frustration and insecurities about being left behind. These could be overcome by being spiritual and practical rather than being deeply religious. Being devoutly religious is a perfectly sane way of life, but when one uses religion and violence to show some of the seven deadly sins he or she has acquired, it only reveals their mental illness. They cannot be indulging in violence if they think society has given them injustice or if they need to create an identity for themselves or if they have a need for belonging, as violence will only further isolate them from the rest of the society. The only way they can achieve their goals is by engaging themselves positively in moderate society and aligning their motives with those of mainstream society. If the simplex-minded, radical-thinking terrorists understood that everything in this world and in life is relative and not absolute, they indeed would bring a better meaning to their lives and the lives of everyone around them.

In the militant organizations, the senior members and leaders recruit immature, uneducated, and unemployed young people with no clear direction in life to the organization. The poor recruits are brainwashed to instill hatred in them, so the militant leaders can carry their agenda. One means for the leaders to carry out their agenda was to preach to their recruits about a manipulated version of martyrdom in which the person acting as a martyr would kill himself or herself and a number of innocent others in a suicide bombing. Teenage kids and young adults were easy targets of the martyrdom preaching, and it is believed that the first suicide bombing carried out in modern history was in 1980, during the Iran-Iraq war when a thirteen-year-old boy strapped grenades to his chest and blew himself up under an enemy tank. Most radical militant leaders call suicide bombings heroic acts that goes to show the insanity of these radical thinkers. Life is not valued as important in some developing countries as it is in most developed countries, so it's easier for teenagers to kill themselves in suicide bombings. Take for example the barbaric teenagers in Pakistan who issued no demands but went on a rampage and killed an unarmed crowd of young police recruits. These pathetic teenagers randomly fired machine guns at the crowd while some of them killed themselves by detonating their suicide belts; they were there only to terrorize future law enforcement recruits so they—in their heads—would have an upper hand in that nation.

These are a confused bunch of misfits who don't understand and care about the basic human right to live and would go to any length to prove something pointless. These idiots should understand that social evolution is not influenced by incapable antisocial eccentrics but rather by social people competing against other groups using their true capabilities. Although a number of radical militant leaders justify suicide bombings by their young followers and 75 percent of people polled in the Middle East a long time ago were in favor, most of their religious leaders are against the tactic. What makes these militants and their leaders hallucinate is still a mystery—are they normal but confused human beings who just don't get the fact that social Darwinism does not mean oppression but rather a freethinker's way of social evolution regardless of race and religion? Or is it due to the inferiority complex of the underdeveloped who think that the developed minds have a superiority complex? Radical thinking does not have anything to do with religion and everything to do with one's perception of life and what one wants to get out of it. Just like when a cult shoots to fame and more people rush to join, a number of copycat militant organizations have emerged in various parts of the developing world. Some people with extreme religious fanaticism in developed countries have been picking up on twisted religious inspirations by extremist leaders like Anwar al-Awlaki. Bad singers don't move to the second round on the music talent show *American Idol*. Similarly, one doesn't want to see fanatics move to the second round acting on their twisted animal instincts and we need more tough judges like Simon to cut the fanatics out.

The governments and societies that these militants live in are already chaotic without them and hence adding the stupid acts of these unsound intellectuals only increase the imbalance. Their one-track mind for creating communist regimes mixed with their radical religious ideologies will only give way to self-inflicted oppression that will ultimately lead to their society's destruction. Unless these incompetent human beings upgrade themselves with their rational-thinking abilities, they are proven to degenerate themselves as their moderate counterparts' acts of sympathy fades away with hard reasoning overriding it. The moderate governments and moderate society should ensure these radical elements don't overtake them. These militants are psychopaths with no moral or ethical constraints who wouldn't hesitate to abuse or kill anybody to achieve their devious agenda. These guys are worse than serial killers in that they have a larger agenda to bring terror to the minds of the entire society. They have low self-esteem and arrested moral and emotional development that makes them easily attracted to charismatic leaders. They could be doing these activities for fame, quick money, or to nurture their rebelliousness and all these people should be given a one-way ticket to either the international space station or Mars, where they can spend their lives with no constraints.

In developed nations, even a small amount of such extreme behavior—as simple as a flag or hand gesture or graffiti that puts down a race or religion or culture—is not tolerated. The mainstream society, including the government and the law enforcement in developing nations, should not tolerate any extreme behavior by militants. Acts of hatred and violence based on race, religion, or any other profile should be condemned and nipped in the bud. But for this to happen, leaders of the mainstream society have to be wise and dynamic individuals who can convince the extremists to choose the right path. Leaders of the mainstream society should be equally passionate and socially responsible to ease the extremists into rehabilitation, so that the mainstream society is not responsible to clean up the extremists' acts of violence and destruction.

It is the responsibility of the mainstream society, including the media, to point out and denounce the irrational thought processes of these extremists, but at the same time the mainstream media personalities should make sure they don't condemn them so much that it incites further hatred from these unreasonable radicals.

Although violence maybe caused by social, biological, and emotional factors in gangs, drug cartels, and terrorists, it is the members of the terrorist groups that are very hard to rehabilitate because they are significantly alienated from the mainstream society and have an enormous social learning disability due to lack of proper social learning ambience. Drug cartel members are tough to rehabilitate because of the lure of the significant amounts of money involved in that trade. Gang members are the easiest of the three to rehabilitate as they are not as alienated as others, money is not a factor, and they are usually punk youths with nothing better to do. One other reason that both drug cartel members and gang members don't leave these lifestyles is the snitch factor that results in members killed as suspected police informants.

If experts are right that aggression and violence stem from human instincts, then all these extremely violent people who are complete social misfits should be hunted down and put in wildlife parks where they can share their violent instincts with their wild animal counterparts. They could put their stupid ideology—survival of the most violent—to the test. One can bet the terrorists wouldn't take the offer to go live on the space station or Mars since they wouldn't have the normal and moderate people to screw around with but only simplex, crazy people like themselves.

From Karl Albrecht's description of simplex thinkers in his book *Practical Intelligence*, it is clear that not all simplex thinkers are terrorists, but all terrorists are simplex thinkers; even better is the idea that not all simplex radical thinkers are terrorists, but all terrorists are simplex radical thinkers. There are a number of simplex radical thinkers who involve themselves in radical activities that may or may not be religious and not harmful to others. It is up to the moderate leaders to shape these simplex radical thinking terrorists on the verge of mental insanity into responsible citizens who lead successful meaningful lives in mainstream society.

Years ago in an interview with Barbara Walters in one of the high security prisons in Israel, a failed Palestinian suicide bomber adamantly blurted that he would go to heaven and be a martyr if he killed all people not of his religion. He vowed that he would try again without hesitation if given a chance. Even some simplex, radical-thinking parents believe this and encourage their kids to be a martyr. For simplex radical-thinking terrorists, every solution is based on religion and only religion. On the other hand, a moderate and dynamic mindset example is that of billionaire real estate mogul Donald Trump, who during an interview on *Larry King Live* offered himself to mediate between Israel and Palestine and resolve their differences for an amicable solution.

Afghanistan, one of world's poorest and least developed countries, has suffered continuous and brutal civil wars. In 1979 the Soviet Union invaded Afghanistan and following the September 11, 2001, World Trade Center attacks, U.S.-led forces invaded Afghanistan and toppled the infamous Taliban government. The Taliban, led by Mullah Mohammed Omar, and Al-Qaeda, led by Osama bin Laden, collaborated during the Taliban's rule of Afghanistan from 1996 to 2001. The Taliban regime in Afghanistan gained diplomatic recognition from only three countries that also provided aid in terms of various supplies to Afghanistan. As the Taliban's power grew, so did people's criticism of its prohibitions like the ban on clapping during sporting events, trimming of beards, and the ban on sports for women. This clearly shows the simple-minded and twisted tricks they played on their people just to be in power and exude control over the country. The Taliban created a new form of Islamic radicalism and did not allow reporters to question or discuss interpretations of their holy book. They banned photography, television, videos, music, dancing, alcohol, pool tables, chess, computers, and video recorders from the public, did not allow politics or political parties, gave no salaries to officials or soldiers, and wanted to live a life like the Prophet who lived fourteen centuries ago.

Although they lived in caves with no TVs or DVD players, it's not about living like the Prophet for these members because the Prophet wouldn't rape women to show his domination and treat them to be illiterate, ignorant pieces of meat who have no love or respect in society. Their caves did not have backyards with barbeque grills but contained torture manuals and tools that they used to drill hands, sever limbs, drag victims, remove eyes, and other mean methods to torture people who disagreed with their simplex minds. Even though they didn't have a bathroom to take a shower or a bar to drink and socialize, they did have training camps with primitive training skills where they trained to be a fighter to attack the enemy and defend themselves. These Neanderthal-living creatures claim that the developed world is materialistic and its citizens not happy because of it. Totally wrong and on the other hand these individuals in the underdeveloped world are not happy, as they are not able to interpret the teachings of a holy book. Money is not the root of all evil but rather it's the frustrations of these Neanderthal beings at not making money like the dynamic-minded beings in the developed world. It is a classic case of fundamentalism gone wrong, with the extremists displaying wrath, envy, and greed for control through violence as a way to vent their frustrations.

These harmful individuals in the underdeveloped world should know that happiness is a state of mind that can be achieved with or without money and igniting violence to suffocate the ones that have it won't provide any results. Instead of wasting time disrupting the lives in the developed world, these primitive fellows should work on improving their own lives to compete technically and economically with the developed world. Competition is fair and square, but confrontation through violent methods only shows their weakness. For Al-Qaeda and Taliban, it's all about control, and they are the ignorant ones who don't want to learn and open up to anything else in this wonderful world other than their twisted version of religion. Their simplex minds can't open up to complex economics or politics of the mainstream society, so their simple but twisted strategy is to create terror and chaos in the society to give them the illusion of control. Women in these societies should not try to join the ranks of these stupid organizations; instead they should better themselves with education and worldly knowledge that will make them loved and respected not by these crooked thugs but other respectable people in the mainstream society.

Of all the heinous crimes committed by the Taliban regime, the worst came in August 1998, when they entered the city of Mazar-i-Sharif and killed everything that moved, including women, children, and animals over two days. A total of eight thousand men, women, children, and animals were killed. This clearly shows that the primitive-minded Taliban government was only about fighting and killing.

After years of warfare with Soviet Union and the Mujahideen, Afghanistan's infrastructure and economy was in shambles. With no running water, no electricity, and no proper roads, one in four children died before the age of five. This is another reason why it is taking so long for the United States to get out of the mess in Afghanistan—it has to tend to the social responsibilities of this region. Although international charities and human rights organizations were trying to help people throughout 1996 to 2001, the Taliban looked at these organizations as if they were trying to corrupt women by trying to uplift them. In 1998 the Taliban closed all the organizations' and UN offices in the country, which meant conditions for citizens deteriorated further.

Unfortunately Afghanistan's top export has been opium, with 90 percent of world's opium supply coming from Afghanistan; it has been claimed that the Taliban, Al-Qaeda, and other militant groups have been using opium money to fund their activities. Drugs and violence won't get them anywhere, and they need to question themselves why not use the opium money to better their people, country, and government? Drug money should never be the source of one's income for the long run, but at least use the drug money to change the country for the better in the short run. Although the U.S. military should have done this a long time ago, finally in 2009, they decided to cut off these terrorists' main source of income that brought them over $300 million a year through extortion and taxation. Why would the Bush government not work on cutting the money source of these terrorists? For the long run the military is funding a $450 million project to give alternatives like wheat cultivation for farmers and improve the infrastructure, so farmers can sell their new crops in a cost effective way.

After the war with Soviets ended, the Afghan rebels, especially Al-Qaeda, felt like the United States had deserted them by simply walking away. After the start of the 1991 Gulf War, Al-Qaeda believed that the United States was trying to setup military bases in all Islamic countries and that might have influenced Al-Qaeda's focus on American interests. The other factor is their unfounded claim of biased U.S. support of Israel. The U.S. supports Israel but wants an unbiased and peaceful solution to the entire issue.

Craziest of all the small-minded militants and terrorists, Osama bin Laden was born to the prestigious and wealthy bin Laden family in Saudi Arabia. The bin Laden family has connections to the Saudi royal family through its huge construction and equity management conglomerate. After Osama spoke publicly against the Saudi government during the 1991 Gulf War, the Saudi government revoked his passport and stripped his citizenship. The bin Laden family disowned Osama for good because of his active involvement with the terrorist organizations. Who would have thought that the son of such wealthy parents and the brother of Harvard alumni would turn out to be such an idiot and disappointment? He has been indicted in the

U.S. court for his alleged involvement in the 1998 U.S. embassy bombings in Africa and is on the FBI's Ten Most Wanted Fugitives list for his involvement in the 2001 World Trade Center attacks. Growing up, he attended school but always liked the after-school Islamic study groups by the Muslim Brotherhood. As a university dropout, he became enamored with a lot of religious lectures from Islamic scholars and later executed the teachings and jihad as the founder of a terrorist network. He is so screwed up that there are claims that he married five times because these women were going to go without marrying anyone, and he married them for the word of God. That was no word of God, but he married these passive women for the simple fact that he could command them at will for cheap thrills.

Some people are slow to learn how to fit into the mainstream society and some never learn. It seems like bin Laden falls into the latter category, as his chronic fanaticism will forever cloud his practical judgments. His stubborn and rebellious attitude, along with twisted religious fanaticism, has taken him from Saudi Arabia to Afghanistan to Sudan to Pakistan. He may have been successful in attacking the World Trade Center towers but his stupid ideology of destroying lives will take him nowhere but hell, and his callous ramblings about religion will soon be forgotten as the works of a deranged and unstable man.

Ten weeks after the 9/11 tragedy, the Pentagon ordered a secret commando unit called the Delta Force to go to Afghanistan and kill bin Laden. What one doesn't understand is that even after the CIA pinpointed bin Laden's location in the mountains using radio intercepts and informants, the commandos didn't get approval to ambush him directly through his back door. There were a number of other ideas by the CIA and the commando unit that would have put them close enough to bin Laden to kill him, but they were again not approved by a higher authority, which can be conveniently assumed as Bush and Cheney. If the Delta Force was sent to capture or kill bin Laden, why not authorize the commandos to take the most convenient route and approach? Were Bush and Cheney pressured by the bin Laden family to save Osama's life? Why would the CIA pay millions of dollars in cash to a militia warlord who thought of bin Laden as a hero to help them get to bin Laden when they had easier way to get to him without paying anybody? So all these questions have no answers except for in the secure hidden files in the White House and Pentagon, and it only makes one believe that the failed Delta Force operation was staged.

Next to Osama in the Al-Qaeda hierarchy is his lieutenant, another "nut case" called Ayman al-Zawahiri, who was once a practicing surgeon and leader of the Egyptian Islamic Jihad (EIJ). Zawahiri was raised in an upper middle class family in Egypt and his parents were well educated and not very religious. Zawahiri became religious because of his uncle's influence, joining the Muslim Brotherhood radical group at an early age and becoming a student of radical thinkers and teachers. One can have genes for moderation from their parents but can still be influenced by religious fanaticism by associating with such people at an early age. When the Egyptian government executed one of Zawahiri's radical-thinking preachers for conspiracy, he formed a group with four of his schoolmates to overthrow the government and later merged his group with EIJ. While he was still active in Jihad group, he served in the Egyptian Army as a surgeon, and then earned his master's degree in surgery. The attempt to overthrow the Egyptian government was disrupted when the government learned of the group's plan and arrested most of its members. But the group was successful in assassinating the president later that year, and Zawahiri was arrested, convicted of dealing weapons, and sent to prison for three years. It's a classic case of a mixture of religious fanaticism and power that should never happen.

After Zawahiri got his master's degree, he married a religious woman and had six children. These socially awkward recluses should never be allowed to get married and have kids because they not only abuse them but also put them in danger because of their dangerous activities. It is in the best interest of everyone that they live by themselves, as they are certainly wasting the lives of innocent people. In search of a partner in crime to fill the void in his life, Zawahiri moved from Egypt to Saudi Arabia to Pakistan and Afghanistan after getting out of prison. He was involved in a number of attacks on innocent people in Egypt, and for his involvement in these attacks, Zawahiri was sentenced to death by the Egyptian government. He is currently on FBI's most wanted list for his involvement in 1998 U.S. embassy bombings in Africa. Now that he has got the fame he was looking for, it is time to enter reality, take responsibility for his actions and stop killing innocent people for nothing. Redemption is soothing, and he will have time to search his soul in jail if he opts to surrender.

While Afghanistan has been in utter chaos, Pakistan has been showing a democratic face on the outside while various governments have continuously abetted terrorist activities. After the attack on the World Trade Center, the U.S. government designated over 300 individuals of different nationalities and organizations as terrorists and terrorist supporters and froze over $130 million in terrorist assets. Although three groups from Pakistan Harkat-ul-Mujahideen (HUM), Lashkar-e-Toiba (LET), and Jaish-e-Mohammad (JEM) have been designated as foreign terrorist organizations, the Pakistan government and the ISI are suspected of notifying these organizations that their bank accounts would be frozen. Although the Pakistan government and the ISI claim that they did not support the Taliban government in Afghanistan, one year's aid was estimated at $30 million in supplies. The three terrorist organizations in the name of Kashmir have tried to create terror in different parts of India with their fundamentalist view and hatred toward other religions. The Pakistani government is making a complete fool of themselves by aiding these terrorist organizations and denying any claims of giving help. HUM claims itself to be a Jihadi organization that provides awareness of Jihad. But this organization also falls under the same category as other terrorist organizations, with a confused agenda involved in kidnapping and killing innocent people during the Soviet-Afghan war and in the Indian state of Kashmir. These below average thugs, with aid from its below average government establishment, have now started terrorist activities in various cities in India in an attempt to display their simple-mindedness. Only in Pakistan and Afghanistan can these terrorists run around freely even after committing a crime as large as hijacking a commercial airplane. It is because of the support from the Pakistani government and the notorious ISI that these rascals have become brazen to commit crimes of such magnitude. What happened after they hijacked an Indian Airlines flight in 1993 in return for the release of three of their fellow terrorists? They are still running around scot-free in Pakistan and Afghanistan, with complete backing from the governments. Don't these governments have any sense of responsibility? It is pathetic to see the governments of these underdeveloped countries to ruin themselves because they are constantly supporting and encouraging these negative elements.

LET is one of the largest and most active militant organizations that was founded in Afghanistan, but it is currently based in Pakistan and operates several militant training camps in Pakistan-occupied Kashmir. As any militant organization, LET members are immature, unruly, and uneducated, and have a radical objective to implement Islamic rule in South Asia, Russia, and China. It has carried out several attacks on innocent people even in Pakistan because they did not like then President Musharraf's policies. Several countries including Pakistan have banned LET, but for Pakistan, it was just an act to appease the rest of the world. Most of LET's activities have been financed by funds collected for charity purposes or from the Pakistani government. During the Kargil War in Kashmir, the Pakistani military, along with militants, including members of LET, crossed the Line of Control and started attacking the Indian military. Then U.S. President Bill Clinton said he was baffled when Pakistan's prime minister rushed to him and asked for U.S. assistance. Clinton asked Pakistan's PM to pull back his forces, along with the militants. Indian military retaliated, recaptured, and gained control of the Line of Control. Pakistan and a number of these terrorist abetting governments believe they can get whatever they want just by smooching the developed world, but it doesn't work that way. They really need to stop abetting the terrorists and then smooch the developed world for some balanced assistance from them.

Because of brutal militant attacks, over a quarter million minority Hindu Pandits in Kashmir have fled to safer Jammu region despite opposition from the local majority moderate Muslims. They slowly moved to other cities in India and have killed thousands of innocent people by bombing random targets in an attempt to get attention. It is the insane and the simplex radicals that have a hard time dealing with social issues and their paranoid mind seeks to find a remote reason to connect every issue to religion.

JEM, launched in 2000, is another militant organization that is a pawn of Pakistan's ISI and has been active mostly in the Indian state of Jammu and Kashmir but lately has been working with other terrorist organizations to create terror in different parts of India. JEM has been endorsed and supported by Pakistan's three religious chiefs, ISI, and various other terrorist organizations. One of the most gruesome incidents by JEM is the kidnapping and murder of American journalist Daniel Pearl in Pakistan. Pearl was working for the *Wall Street Journal* as the South Asia bureau chief and was investigating the case of shoe bomber Richard Reid. Since he was also investigating the links between Al-Qaeda and Pakistan's ISI, the militants mistook him for a

CIA agent. In January 2002, he went to Pakistan to conduct his investigations and was kidnapped on his way to interview a sheikh. In return for his release, the militants demanded that the United States release all Pakistani terror detainees and continue its shipment of F-16 fighter jets to Pakistan. I almost fell of the chair laughing when I read these stupid terrorists' demands. What a cheap thrill it must have been for the militants to have a commanding position to negotiate and have their way with the superpower. Of course, the United States did not negotiate with the militant group. After nine days, the increasingly agitated militants killed Pearl by slashing his throat; they videotaped his murder and released it to the public. Two weeks later the journalist's body, cut into ten pieces, was found buried in a shallow grave on the outskirts of the city. Within a year, suspects in the killing were arrested and sentenced to death mainly because of pressure from the developed world. Former Pakistan president Musharraf claims in his book that Pearl was murdered by a British intelligence agent but doesn't provide any proof to back it up because there wouldn't be any. Seriously, the deranged mindset of a president who has been an ally in the war against terrorism should raise eyebrows in the U.S. Congress. The Pakistani government is only exploiting the United States for the massive amount of aid it is receiving. The United States and its allies should take a second look into these so called supporting governments because they are clearly not holding their end of the bargain as terrorists are freely running around in these countries.

Ever since Saddam Hussein invaded Kuwait in 1990, accusing Kuwait of stealing Iraq's oil through slant drilling, it was the beginning of his end. This was a wrong move by the former authoritarian that ultimately led to his removal from office and execution. His radical nature was molded early in his life by his maternal uncle who was a militant Iraqi and took these ideals further by playing a key role in the 1968 coup to bring his Baath Party to power. Saddam started off strong modernizing the Iraqi economy, but somewhere along the way greed took over. Saddam established compulsory free education and illiteracy eradication campaigns, and diversified the economy by developing other industries, but he was also a man who was insecure about losing his grip on power, his people, and the country. Once he had an autocratic grip on the nation, he started taunting his neighbors, resulting in life-long wars for this ruler. In 1980, he instigated the war with Iran by attacking Iran's embassy in London, asking for autonomy of the Arab majority oil rich southern Iranian region with the help of homegrown terrorists. In eight years of fighting that followed, the two countries not only destroyed most of each other's oil industry, but Iraq also used mustard gas and sarin nerve gas to kill more than 100,000 Iranians. This ruthless dictator also used these chemical weapons in Iraq's northern state of Kurdistan and ran concentration camps where as many as 200,000 Kurds died.

Unstable and insecure dictators are an economic disaster not only for the country they are ruling but also for their neighbors as Saddam showed it in 1990 by invading Kuwait. He accused the neighbor of illegally drilling oil, although he was trying to get rid of the $14 billion war debt that he had to pay his neighbor. Smart leaders thrive, but conniving leaders fall hard. That's what happened when he declared Kuwait to be part of Iraq so he could acquire its oil industry. UN sanctions against Iraq resulted in the deaths of over half a million children, but the dictator and his two notorious sons lived happily and lavishly in their palaces. The entire saga came to an end in 2003 when Saddam's regime was toppled and each and everyone, including his two sons, were killed or put on trial. Both sons were infamous for the rape and murder of numerous Iraqi women, and for killing numerous army officers who did not obey them.

Although the reason for coalition forces invading Iraq has been controversial, it is justified by the fact that establishing a safe and secure government in Iraq is required for stability in the region. The occupation of Iraq by the coalition forces led to the insurgency by Al-Qaeda and other terrorist organizations, attacks targeted at the coalition forces, Iraqi security forces, Iraqi civilians, and foreign contractors aimed at creating terror, destabilizing the government, and driving the coalition forces out of Iraq. If not for the insurgency, the new Iraqi government would have been stronger and better able to build the infrastructure and economy so badly needed in the postwar period. These militants and their supporters are so radical and eccentric in their beliefs that they condemn democracy and believe that participants in Iraq's elections are enemies of Islam. They are mostly illiterate, unemployed people who are full of hatred and slow to learn the importance of stability and economic growth. But for this to happen, moderate leaders in those nations should take necessary steps to teach the militants about the workings of the mainstream society.

Militant organizations have sprung up denser and faster than mushrooms during the rainy season in the Middle East, and both have been regarded as tasteless and useless to the society in general. Hezbollah came into existence when Israel invaded Lebanon in 1982 in response to the assassination attempt on Israel's ambassador to the United Kingdom. The assassination attempt was believed to be the work of a Palestinian terrorist organization, and Israel attacked PLO based in Lebanon. Ayatollah Khomeini's followers created the Hezbollah organization to spread the Islamic revolution that occurred in Iran, and the militants joined the ongoing Lebanese civil war, which started in 1975, to drive the PLO out of Lebanon.

The United States and a number of other developed nations have blacklisted Hezbollah as a terrorist organization. At the height of its activity, Hezbollah was involved in suicide attacks, assassinations, kidnappings—all aimed at Israeli civilians and soldiers. Peace and terrorist organizations are mutually exclusive and usually family and friends of these terrorists are to blame for infusing deep hatred into their minds. Unlike terrorist organizations like Al-Qaeda, which has been trying to get all over the map, Hezbollah has always been based in and around Lebanon. Hezbollah, Hamas, and the PLO fighting against Israel have even asked Al-Qaeda not to intervene in their fight. These simplex, radical-thinking militants cannot comprehend the fact that Israel and Palestinians have the right to coexist and were strongly opposed to any final peace deal between the two during the 1993 peace process, accusing then PLO chief Arafat of neglecting Palestinian interests. The paranoid Hezbollah militants showed the extent of their hatred in 1996 and asked for the boycott of the movie *Independence Day* since the movie depicts a Jewish scientist who helps save the world from alien invasion. Hatred has been constantly fed into the minds of these clueless militants, and it has become not just a state of mind but more like a sickness or a disease that no doctor can cure. It is claimed that one of the Hezbollah leaders said that Hezbollah would not have to go against Jews worldwide if they all gathered in Israel. But the question is wouldn't Israel be another superpower if all Jews were to gather in Israel? Wouldn't that make the terrorists even weaker? In developing and underdeveloped countries, creating terror is not just limited to religious fanatics.

Even a tiny developing island country of Sri Lanka was not spared by the militants who waged a violent secessionist campaign there for over three decades. The campaign, which amounted to nothing but the deaths of innocent people, reached its final chapter with the death of the founder and leader of the militant organization. The militants in Sri Lanka were fighting for an autonomous independent state and attacking only people who actively opposed it. One cannot act as a militant outfit and expect to win a resistance movement. They chose to be a militant outfit fighting a bloody protracted civil war by funding their campaign with illegal activities like narcotics and extortion.

The enmity between the two ethnic groups started during the pre-colonial period, when a number of Tamil kings from India invaded Sri Lanka and ruled for a while. The British favored the minority Tamils over the majority Sinhalese, which escalated tensions. This is a perfect example that a minority community that wants to take part in the day-to-day mainstream society activities must show its capabilities, and once they turn violent to show their frustrations, they are doomed. The senseless killings between the two ethnic groups continued, as a small Tamil boy called Prabhakaran watched from the sidelines. The constant violence shaped his political views, and at the age of eighteen, he formed the militant group Liberation Tigers of Tamil Elam (LTTE).

Even in the midst of violence if this young boy had been given constant guidance on the ill effects of violence and the power of diplomatic struggle, his views could have been changed. To achieve change, one has to rise above the occasion and negotiate success by compromising rather than harping on a simplex-minded goal and refusing to compromise. Prabhakaran chose to uphold his rebellious attitude and started assassinating prominent political figures who he thought were obstructing his path toward his goal. Even when the Sri Lankan government offered Prabhakaran a chance to go to the negotiation table, he was unwilling to budge from his goal. Power, control, and notoriety had gotten into his head, and he was constantly enlarging his goal, trying to take on more than he could. On two occasions, once in 1987 and again in 2001, a resolution to provide certain degree of regional autonomy was so close to adoption, but both times the LTTE rejected it, claiming certain critical issues. If the militant group chief had accepted the resolution on one of the two occasions, a chapter in Sri Lankan history would have been closed on a positive note, but fate had other plans. The Sri Lankan government was nice enough to provide regional autonomy to the militants and the minority community, but the militant leader was just looking for vengeance. What is the point in fighting if all you want to do is go down fighting and not fight for a cause? Even if they had accepted regional autonomy, like many other militant groups because of their volatile nature, they wouldn't have been able to hold it together. Rebels all over the world using violence to build autonomous regions should learn from Charles Wesley Mumbere who is currently the king of Rwenzururu kingdom in Uganda. After his father's death, he and his followers who had been fighting for autonomy laid down their weapons and Charles moved to the U.S. and built a career for himself as a nurse saving lives. He waited for two decades until the Ugandan government formally recognized his kingdom when he moved back to his native country to take care of his people.

German concentration camps and their heinous acts of genocide during World War II are being left out in this book since they have cleaned up their act and have been one of the most developed countries, with moderate communal values; its not about trying to downplay what they did in the concentration camps during World War II, but its all behind us now.

Some of the African countries are still the poorest countries in the world, with the worst mindset involving them in genocide instead of alleviating the standard of living and helping their fellow countrymen. Reading the stories of the tribes in Africa will make you realize how far back in social structure era are they living in. Although they are not religiously fanatic, they are territorial tribal fanatics who are like most other fanatics—uneducated, unemployed, too much idle time on their hands, and looking to fill a void in their life. The continent itself has been alienated because of its geographic location and widespread natural calamities, but more than that it is the utter lack of strong governments in the countries. Lack of strong government has trickled down to lack of infrastructure and lack of businesses, so the economy is down the drain. That has led to lawlessness wilder than its lions.

Three tribes in Rwanda, the Tutsi, the Twa (minority tribes), and the Hutu (majority tribe) make up this culturally beautiful country, but the negative energy flow mainly between the Tutsis and the Hutus. The conflict between Hutus and Tutsis goes back to 1972, when an estimated 300,000 Hutus were killed in the nation of Burundi; in 1993, after Tutsi militia assassinated the Hutu president of Burundi, Hutu extremists killed about 400,000 Tutsis. If you thought I must have gotten the years and number of killed wrong, no I did not get it wrong, and I agree these numbers are staggering for this time and age but these people still live in the stone-age era of no law no government. In the midst of the country's ongoing civil war, in April 1994, President Habyarimana was returning to Rwanda in the presidential jet along with some of his ministers and the president of Burundi Cyprien Ntaryamira. Out of nowhere a surface-to-air missile hit the jet's wing, followed by another that hit the tail. The flaming jet crashed into the presidential palace garden, killing all nine passengers. The Hutu extremists blamed the Tutsis for the attack while the Tutsis blamed it on the French government, which was backing the Hutus. Over the next 100 days, Hutus were killing Tutsis randomly all over the country.

When people are uneducated, unemployed, and in abject poverty, it is easier for people to engage themselves in mindless violence just by a deadly dose of hatred. At the end of the 100 days, close to a million Tutsis were brutally killed and about 100,000 moderate Hutus were also killed for backing the peace accord. The RPF units in Kigali and their comrades from the north came together and took over the Hutu regime in Rwanda and stopped the genocide. Once the Tutsis were back in power in Rwanda, about 2 million Hutus in fear of Tutsi retaliation fled Rwanda to neighboring countries where thousands died of diseases caused by poor hygiene in refugee camps.

Didn't the Hutus have any sense when they were killing mindlessly? Aren't they aware of the phrase what goes around comes around? Guess not, since they still live in the stone-age period. The people who started the killing should be put to death without sparing a soul. Then U.S. president Bill Clinton flew to Kigali later and apologized to the people of Rwanda for the world community's inaction during the genocide. But it is understandable that fear of getting killed while in the middle of it in a lawless country was the main reason for the inaction. Sometimes inaction is better than any positive action from the international community, so that these underdeveloped countries learn to take responsibility for their actions and understand that aid is not the answer for their stupidity.

Another conflict in Africa is in the western Sudan region of Darfur between the Sudanese military and the Arab militia group called Janjaweed on one side and the non-Arab rebel groups, including the Sudan Liberation Movement (SLM), Justice and Equality Movement (JEM) on the other side. The camel herding, cattle herding and farming militant groups in this drought-affected, full-fledged desert region attacked on the ground looting, raping, and killing a lot of the population. For about seven months, the militia executed the villagers and burned down entire villages, forcing the surviving two million non-Arabs to flee Darfur. Some prisoners were axed to death, and some of them were crucified on the prison wall with nails hammered to the forehead or the chest. Most of the refugee camps have substandard conditions and feature mud huts and plastic tents with substandard hygienic conditions. If people wander away from these refugee camps, even in search of livelihood, they risk of getting looted, raped, or even killed by the militia. The militia still wanders the streets and sometimes put witnesses in prison after the International Criminal Court investigated the entire genocide incident and charged a number of ministers and top militia commanders with human rights atrocities.

You hear about all the slaughter, your face turns serious, and you sit there wondering why in the hell do these monsters deserve to live in this world? We don't want to make Africa the Louisiana or the Oakland of this wonderful world and need to come up with better strategies for this place to get rid of this genocide decease rather than just supplying aid after the fact. These hot-blooded deadly creatures have made a habit of battling at least one civil war at a time, and it's hard to tell if it's a weird display of their testosterone or backwardness. Every nation in the continent wants to jump into a civil war and eight of them got involved in the Second Congo War, along with a countless number of militia groups. Sometimes they get involved to help their friends in neighboring countries but mostly to loot the hidden treasures of diamonds, cobalt, and gold located in the vast mines.

The Second Congo War happened between 1998 and 2003 and caused the deaths of five million and millions more to take refuge in neighboring countries. Classified as the biggest war in modern African history, it left thousands of people dying daily from diseases caused by starvation and poor sanitary conditions in refugee camps and villages. Again the Hutus and the Tutsis were up against each other killing mindlessly while fueled by hate messages broadcast over the radio. Everybody was eyeing the abundant natural resources worth billions of dollars, and even one-time allies from neighboring governments were fighting each other during a ceasefire in an attempt to gain control of these mines. The grotesque part of the war is that these deranged and underdeveloped human beings hunted and ate the African Pygmies, alleging that their flesh had magical powers.

Can one believe that the First Sudanese War went on from 1955 till 1972, and after an eleven-year recuperation, they were at it again, battling the Second Sudanese War in 1983? What kind of a warmonger and a blood-sucking vampire do you have to be to instigate a second civil war for another twenty-two years that kills two million people and displaces twice that number? The president was so thirsty for blood that he decided to institute the Sharia Law in the autonomous southern region, and that led the non-Arabic rebel group to fight the government against its implementation. Mixing religion and government is a bad idea, and in a lawless underdeveloped country with poor strategies of any kind, it is a definite no-no. Instead of negotiating with the south to share the abundant water and oil resources available there, the leaders of this underdeveloped nation decided to take full control by implementing laws that they knew would start a conflict. It is pathetic that the African continent has become the black hole (no pun intended) of the world, where generations have been lost with no educational opportunities or health care services to millions of people. It is sad to see the underdeveloped leaders of the continent are not able to perceive the depth of the situation and react accordingly. The wildlife in Africa is tame compared to these monstrous human beings, and it is these untamed animal instincts that have kept foreign investments out of the continent for fear of their safety. To put things in perspective, that continent will be underdeveloped forever unless there is a significant shift in their approach to even basic things in life. Fear of safety is not only evident by the lack of foreign investments but also the lack of the UN and other international charitable communities during civil wars. Even though the charitable organizations wanted to help the hoards of starved and unhealthy victims, safety was the main concern. Finally they decided to risk their lives and drop hundreds of thousands of tons of food and other services.

Conclusion

All references made to developed minds and developing minds in this book are mostly based on the developed country the United States and the developing country India. The structure and system in other developed and developing counterparts may or may not be better than the depiction in this book.

The developed countries are made up of visionaries, both in the government and private sector, that set certain standards—much higher than in developing countries—for citizens to follow and abide by as an employee or owner or as a family. GDP is predominantly made up of services and industrial sectors, with a small share from the agricultural sector. These countries maintain a high human development index, and the government tries to keep taxes, inflation, unemployment, and population under poverty low while maintaining a sustainable and high-growth economy. Most people in developed countries have a dynamic mindset and give utmost value to personal development while still maintaining family values, recreational activities, and other beliefs including religious.

The developing countries are made up of visionaries, both in the government and private sector that have set much lower standards than in developed countries for citizens to follow and abide by as an employee or owner or as a family. These visions may not be as high as that of developed minds due to various socioeconomic variables, which should be overcome in order to achieve the best they can. Moving away from a simplex-thinking mindset to a dynamic mindset would help them accept change that will help overcome the socioeconomic issues that are hampering creation an environment favoring personal development while maintaining family values, recreational activities, and other beliefs. The government needs to create an atmosphere for human development index growth while keeping the population under poverty low, along with taxes, inflation, and unemployment. The low-yielding agriculture should be changed to provide high yields while the industrial and services sector growth should be encouraged with a plan to implement the growth.

The stupid terrorists need to change their simplex, radical-thinking mindset and mold themselves into the common vision of their mainstream moderate government leaders. They should help build the already shattered economy and infrastructure instead of fighting against the government. They need to understand that all issues and differences can be resolved diplomatically without violence. This can be achieved by keeping the mind occupied in various activities such as positive personal development—that's not religion based—education, career, family, recreational activities, and moderate beliefs both religious and secular.

Concerted efforts at various levels from all the minds need to happen to make this world a better place for future generations.